BEING YOUR OWN BOSS

To own and manage your own business is the greatest and most satisfying challenge in the business world. The odds are against you, but you can survive and succeed—*if.*

If you act like a pro and not an amateur. *If* you learn how to deal with banks and lawyers, accountants and investors, suppliers and customers, employees and advertising men. *If* you're willing to work hard and use your intelligence and common sense to achieve the most satisfying experience in business— the independence of being your own boss.

The author of this book has been a highly successful businessman for many years. Now he has put down in hard-hitting, plain-spoken language what he has learned and what you need to know if you want to take the plunge and reap the rewards.

HOW TO START AND MANAGE YOUR OWN BUSINESS

Third Edition

Gardiner G. Greene

A MENTOR BOOK

MENTOR
Published by the Penguin Group
Penguin Books USA Inc., 375 Hudson Street,
New York, New York 10014, U.S.A.
Penguin Books Ltd, 27 Wrights Lane,
London W8 5TZ, England
Penguin Books Australia Ltd, Ringwood,
Victoria, Australia
Penguin Books Canada Ltd, 2801 John Street,
Markham, Ontario, Canada L3R 1B4
Penguin Books (N.Z.) Ltd, 182-190 Wairau Road,
Auckland 10, New Zealand

Penguin Books Ltd, Registered Offices:
Harmondsworth, Middlesex, England

First Mentor Printing, September, 1975
First Mentor Printing (Third Edition), August, 1987
12 11 10 9 8 7 6 5 4

 REGISTERED TRADEMARK—MARCA REGISTRADA

Printed in the United States of America

PUBLISHER'S NOTE
This publication is designed to provide accurate and authoritative information in regard
to the subject matter covered. It is sold with the understanding that the publisher is no
engaged in rendering legal, accounting or other professional service. If legal advice o
other expert assistance is required, the service of a competent professional person shoul
be sought.

I gratefully acknowledge the encouragement and help provided me by Patrick Jackson and his late wife Miriam Jackson, and also, more recently, from the author Matthew Braun.

G.G.G.

Contents

CONTENTS

Part Three: Management Tips

Part Four: Constructive Thinking

Part Five: Cautionary Thinking

Foreword

The purpose of this book is to help small businessmen. I am not an author or even a writer; I am a businessman. I am trying to share with you some of my ideas, experiences, and techniques. Businessmen should communicate more with one another and so learn from each other's experiences. All other professionals do.

This book is critical of some of the vendors and professionals we deal with, explaining why bankers, lawyers, accountants, insurance, and advertising men act and feel the way they do toward small business. Businessmen should understand these people, and this book suggests ways of dealing with them more effectively.

You may desire to have your own business. If you are now employed, this book may help you stay where you are, with a safe nine-to-five job. After reading this, you may appreciate how lucky you are working for someone else.

Or—if you decide to become a gambler and have plenty of guts and patience (some ability also necessary) and really want your fortune, some of the suggestions here may help.

This is not a textbook. It is a compilation of ideas that may be helpful. I have tried to dig into some of the major problems rather than cover every possible one with generalizations. To make it handy, subheads and indented paragraphs enable you quickly to refer to the highlights.

The conflict between big and small business is not simple. Each has its place in our society. The small businessman must know survival techniques in a big-business-oriented world. As in other professions, he must keep his skills and methods up to date. He has chosen the many privileges of independence and cannot expect anyone else to do more than hold his coat while he does the fighting.

I am familiar with much of the statistical and published material on small business. Some of it is quoted here. A scientific study of these is not my purpose. Such arm's-length, academic treatment of small business is prevalent in the literature that has been written *about* small business.

My relation to small business is not arm's length, nor academic, but intimate—with some failures and some successes. I am engaged in it every day and have been for over thirty years.

If I have erred in this book, it is on the side of practical overstatement in which my working experience may have caused overemphasis.

Professors can give us a more balanced treatment from a historical perspective. They are writing *about* small business. I am writing *for* it—and the sturdy men and women who labor, prosper, fail, and labor again in its practice.

GARDINER G. GREENE

PART ONE

FINANCIAL STRATEGIES

*"Success is a journey,
not a destination"*

CHAPTER I

Amateur or Pro

WELCOME to the world of small business, fellow gamblers!

If you have plenty of guts and patience, and are willing to work long, hard hours—plus some degree of luck and ability—you may end up playing for the highest stakes in the world.

That is why small business attracts the entrepreneur at heart. The one who gladly trades retirement benefits and pension plans for a shot at his own private roller coaster.

After thirty years up and down the ladder at old Hard Knocks U., that observation is not made lightly. The world of the small business is a lot of fun, but it is no joking matter. Still, there is always the money. Not to mention capital gains and a lifetime absolutely free of drudgery, boredom, and humdrum routine.

Before pursuing that line of thought too closely, though, let's make sure you are heading down the right path. To speed your decision we must first propose a question.

Exactly what is small business?

The answer is neither simple nor readily definable. It is confused, complicated, and constantly changing.

A leading banker in the Northeast says a small businessman is one who wants to become a Big Businessman. Very enlightening.

Inc. Magazine, a prestigious magazine addressed to small businesses, defines its audience as companies with $25 million or less in annual revenue.

The law that established the Small Business Administration (Small Business Act, P.L. 536, 85th Congress, 2d Session) says in Section 3 that a small business "shall be deemed to be one which is independently owned and operated and which is not dominant in its field of operations."

The law defining small business was left deliberately vague, in recognition that the growth of our economy constantly changes the nature of what is small business.

Today the SBA uses four criteria to determine whether or not a specific business qualifies for the prefix "small":

1. Number of employees
2. Dollar sales volume
3. Type of business
4. Nature of business within the industry

A manufacturing business is automatically "small" if it employs less than 50 people, but the criteria is different in each specific industry. For example, American Motors (25,000 employees) qualifies as small because it has less than a 5% market share. A steel rolling mill is small with less than 2,500; a household appliance make is small with less than 500 workers.

In non-manufacturing industries the SBA relies primarily on dollar sales volume. For example, retail and service businesses are small with volumes under $7,500,000; wholesalers are small with volumes under $22,000,000.

The bottom line is, check with your regional Small Business Administration office to get the details on the current qualifications in your specific business.

Fortune magazine, in a 1958 book compiled from a

series of articles, defined small business only on the criterion of the man who operates the company. In their preface to *Adventures in Small Business*, *Fortune*'s editors noted that the articles described businesses run by entrepreneurs and added:

> *Fortune* has arbitrarily set some limits on the dictionary meaning of entrepreneur; for instance, when a man builds a business and then sells out, taking a capital gain and long-term management contract, he is selling the breed short and becoming in effect a hired manager. The true entrepreneur would hock his wife's jewels and sell the company convertible before he would think of working for anyone but himself.

A true small business is one run by that kind of man, they imply. Note that the editors of this big-business publication recognize the difference between the professional businessman and the professional executive, a distinction that will be clarified shortly.

Even this small sampling of the many definitions illustrates the lack of agreement on what constitutes small business. Assets, sales volume, employees, management group, and the owner himself have been suggested as criteria. Another way to arrive at a definition is to compare small business with big business.

Among the factors characterizing big business is its inability to make decisions rapidly or to move fast once they are made. Big companies are heavily weighted with staff people whose function is to make the decisions that line executives carry out. The number of employees involved means that mountains of reports must be generated and digested before decisions can be made.

Small business doesn't have many staff people and can, therefore, make decisions and act on them with lightning speed. This is undoubtedly *a major strength of smallness*. But neither does small business have the funds or the research and development capability of big business.

When big businesses need money, they crank up their printing press and run off a few more stock or bond certificates. Small businesses, even when they are corporations, cannot do this because there is no established market for their stock.

Franchising also tells us something about the primary characteristics of small business. Often the parent companies are big businesses with ample financing, stock market listing, famous national brand products, and large specialized staffs. Despite all this, they choose to franchise local outlets. They have everything it takes to operate company-owned branches, but don't. Why?

The reason is that no hired manager, or home-office representative, can supply the care a local owner will. In service businesses, which most franchises are, this is the crux of the matter. Big business has an advantage only in items which can be centralized, mass-produced, and completely routinized. Processing the food products for a chain of franchised restaurants, for example, fits the abilities of big business. Operating each outlet, with its individual customer requirements and local preferences and peculiarities, does not.

The fact that a small business is of and for the local community is a distinct advantage, and one that big business cannot match.

Beneath all the jargon and semantics, there is one characteristic that applies to any true small-business enterprise. It is run by a pro!

The owner is independent in the sense that he has freedom to do something else beside mere daily operation of the company. He is free to start his second and third businesses, for instance.

What we really mean when we say "small business" may be "independent business," or a company run by an independent owner or small group. If a company gets too big, the owner loses much of his freedom to do other things. He loses his independence. He becomes tied to a company just as surely as a small businessman who falls in love with his business. Or he becomes just a hired manager, despite his stock holdings.

The only factor that remains constant in any size small business is the extent of control the owners can—and do—retain. Thus a publicly held corporation, even one with low assets, probably doesn't qualify as small business because it has not one owner but several. Even if one man owns a majority of stock, it is still difficult for him to both operate the company and retain his independence in the face of demands by stockholders and, increasingly, by government.

Companies with sales exceeding $25 million, more than 500 employees, and assets over $10 million cease to be small businesses—not because of the figures but because it is impossible for a single owner, or small group of owners, to retain operational control without sacrificing their independence. The fun of starting other companies is denied them because they haven't the freedom, the time. They cease being professional businessmen and become professional executives.

What really makes a company a small business is the fact its owner is a man with the freedom, independence, and control to do exactly as he pleases. He has a greater opportunity to make his million than anyone else, but he lives perilously close to failure at all times. What may actually define a small business is that it is a constant gamble. But if it is like Monte Carlo on a shoestring, at least it is one forever operated by that *pro* mentioned earlier.

That brings us down to another knotty little problem. Many small businessmen are amateurs, not professionals.

You can tell in an instant the difference between an amateur or pro on the golf course. Yet many haven't applied the same yardstick to their own field.

What is a pro businessman? One who is in business in general. Who doesn't care whether he is in armatures or artichokes, or both. Whose goal is to make a profit. For whom business itself is a challenge and a game. A man who enjoys it more than food or women or any other diversion.

The professional businessman can be compared, for example, with a machinist who is in that field because he loves the work. It is both vocation and avocation, from which, incidentally, he hopes to make a living. The pro is a businessman *only* coincidentally, simply because that happens to be the name of the game with the highest stakes.

The differences between these two are obvious, however. If there were suddenly no more need for machinists, one of them would be out of business. A pro businessman, on the other hand, would simply switch to some other product. The basic techniques he uses would not change—only the details and the terminology of the particular industry would be altered. The machinist, unfortunately, would have to learn an entirely new trade. The distinction might be termed that of entrepreneur as contrasted to artisan.

If you are crazy about metal-working, fine. Set up a hobby shop in your basement. But don't try to make your living at it. That is, don't if you want to be a businessman.

Artistry such as metal-working gives us our great craftsmen, and there is much to be said for that. It is just that in the world of small business a person is basically either/or. Choose now, before you get halfway down the wrong track. If you are a craftsman, why bother trying to run a business organization? Chances are you'll botch it. It is difficult enough for a seasoned pro, let alone an amateur. Instead, work as an independent, a professional in your own specialized craft. That is one decision you will never regret.

But if at heart you are a businessman, then cut the cards and ante up. Nothing is wild except the dealer.

Before you decide to bet the limit, however, ask yourself one final question. Can you honestly say you are a professional? There are four basic criteria.

1. *The professional businessman is not tied to any particular industry.* When asked what he does, he doesn't say, "jeweler." Rather he says, "businessman" or "in my own business." He *couldn't* say jeweler because he is probably also in real estate, manufacturing, and other businesses.

If you think of yourself primarily as a jeweler, cash in your chips and call it a night.

2. *The business professional starts companies, products, developments, and projects as well as running them.* He does not act as a conservator or trustee of a going business. Standing still is going backwards, and he knows it. Therefore, he is seldom a hired manager who simply executes plans and policies decided by others. Such men are necessary and important. They may be highly experienced, able, and making $200,000 a year. But they are different from professional businessmen. They are professional *executives.*

What separates the two is that the executives are not taking the risk. Someone else is, and paying them a comfortable salary. Many of these hired executives are serving their apprenticeship. As soon as they acquire the experience, capital, and guts they will be out on their own. Then they might become professional businessmen.

3. *The professional businessman is a master of the techniques and methods of his profession.* Most likely he has a natural aptitude for them, an innate skill in applying them. Even if he doesn't, he understands all parts of the management mix and keeps up on developments just as a doctor, lawyer, accountant, or other professional. He is more apt to be heard talking about marketing psychology or employee incentives than about machinery and suppliers' lines.

He can learn to operate in any particular field overnight, because he knows the objectives and techniques are constant—only details vary.

4. *Professionalism implies a concern for the community in which the businessman operates.* Being a professional means more than just devoting full time to a job. If it didn't, everyone connected in any way with business would be a professional businessman—from janitors and file clerks up.

Being a doctor requires dedication to the Hippocratic Oath in addition to having technical training and ability. Lawyers are dedicated to the ideals of justice and a government of laws.

The professional businessman doesn't have, at this time, any formal licensing or organizational requirements to meet. His ethical and moral concern for his field of endeavor as well as his community is no less real, however.

The word "businessman" ought to be a term of respect and attainment, like doctor, lawyer, philosopher, poet, or professor, for ours is a business-based economy. These people and everyone else in our society are economically dependent on the businessman's output. The pro recognizes this responsibility and channels some part of his organization's energy into bettering the community.

The scoring system on this self-quiz is quite simple. If you can't stand to work for someone else, and have an uncontrollable itch to make a million, you may be a pro.

Should you decide to take the plunge, you might one day become an entrepreneur juggling corporations and capital gains with true legerdemain. Perhaps you might even become an industrialist or tycoon.

But in the world of small business, labels are unimportant. Promoter? Industrialist? Entrepreneur? Tycoon? All meaningless. The game is what counts, and the way it is played is what separates the sheep from the lambs. *The pros from the amateurs.*

Welcome aboard, fellow gamblers. The play is fast and the rules loose. The secret is in knowing when to check or bet.

And how to raise a stake.

CHAPTER II

Financing a New Business

ORGANIZING a small business is easy—anyone can do it. But there is a knack to doing it right. The first consideration is what organizational form you will give this burgeoning venture.

This is a critical decision because it affects your liability for the business and the taxes you must pay. It's a good idea to review these options with your accountant and tax attorney before committing yourself.

Sole proprietorship is the simplest form, but it carries some very complex liabilities. *John Doe, Prop.* That's a shingle we've all seen in one variation or another along the Main Streets of small towns around the country. *Proprietor.* It means that you and only you are running the show. It's a simple structure. You can just set up shop and open for business (complying, of course, with whatever licensing or statutory requirements apply). You can operate in any fashion that pleases you, with no need to report to partners, directors, or shareholders.

Sole proprietorship also means that you and only you are completely responsible—to the full extent of your personal net worth—for the liabilities of the business. Insurance coverage can be obtained to restrict some of the risks, and liability on some contracts can be limited to your business assets. But if you're engaged in litigation, whether for negligence or in a contract dispute, court judgments can reach all of your personal assets. And if you need capital beyond your personal assets, you're out of luck. You can't sell shares in a proprietorship. Nor can a proprietorship outlive its founder. You can will the assets to your heirs, but if you want to make sure the business will continue, this structure doesn't make that possible.

All income of the business will be considered your personal income and taxed accordingly, at ordinary income rates. (Proprietorships report income and expenses on Schedule C of Form 1040.) Under the Tax Reform Act of 1986, the applicable tax rates in years after 1987 are either 15% (on incomes below $17,850 for single people and $29,750 for married couples filing jointly) or 28%.

The income tax advantage of a sole proprietorship is that you're only taxed once on your business income. If you own a corporation (with the exception of a subchapter S corporation, discussed below), the profits of the business are taxed at corporate rates; then the money you take out of the business is taxed again at ordinary income rates.

The disadvantage of a sole proprietorship is that the only income shifting of tax-shelter advantage is a Keogh Plan for retirement savings. If you employ others in your business, the amount of money you can contribute to the retirement plan on your own behalf is no greater than the contribution you make to each of your employees.

Perhaps the major drawback, however, of an individual proprietorship is the management consideration. With no one else to fall back on, with no one else to share decision-making or to whom to delegate authority, the business reflects—nay, magnifies—the weaknesses of its owner. Unless you are extremely well-organized, efficient, and resourceful, the sole proprietorship presents a bushel of potential headaches.

Partnership. A partnership is an association of two or more persons carrying on the same trade or business; each contributes money, property, labor, or skill, and each shares in the profits and losses. It is a consensual organization: each partner may act on behalf of the partnership and bind it contractually, and each is entitled to participate in the day-to-day decisions, subject to the rights and obligations of each partner as defined by a "partnership agreement" drawn up to form the organization. Partnership is the form of organization used by most law and investment banking firms.

Like a sole proprietorship, a partnership does not pay taxes. The partnership reports its income (on Form 1065), but each partner is taxed on his or her share of the profits, capital gains, losses, reductions and credits. All profits, even those retained in the business, must be declared as income.

Unlike sole proprietorships, partnerships have some ability to control tax benefits and liabilities for the greatest benefits of the partners. Partners could agree, for example, that one partner is liable for 30% of the losses, yet has a claim to only 20% of the ordinary income and 5% of the capital gains. A partnership can lease or buy property or borrow money from its partners, resulting in interest income to the partners and tax deductions for the partnership. A partner can sell property to the partnership, creating a taxable gain or loss to the partner, and thus avoid the disparity between tax basis and fair market value if it had been contributed to the partnership as capital.

But the responsibilities of a general partner are enormous. He or she is liable not only for his own business decisions and losses, but also for those of all the co-partners as well. And since any partner can bind all the others legally, the liability can be enormous.

The Tax Reform Act of 1986 stripped certain types of partnerships of some of the advantages they enjoyed under the old tax laws. Under the old law, limited partnerships (in which one or more general partners managed the business and shared legal and financial responsibilities while limited partners confined their participation to the investment they made) flourished as "tax shelters" because limited partners could use losses from the partnership to offset any other income. Under the new law, however, losses from a limited partnership may only be used only to offset losses from other "passive" investments, in which the investor has only a financial interest. These losses may no longer be used to offset income from employment, interest income, etc.

The new tax law also eliminated most of the advantages of family partnerships, which were formerly used to shift taxable income by allocating income between parents and children. Under the Tax Reform Act of 1986, any income received by children under age 14 in excess of $1,000 is taxed at the parents' higher tax rate.

Corporations. Corporations of all kinds are the most flexible business structures, providing shareholders (owners) with almost total protection from personal liability and with the most latitude in tax planning. A corporation is a separate taxable and legal entity from its owner(s). Shareholders are rarely liable for the losses or obligations of the corporation beyond the corporation's own assets.

The Tax Reform Act of 1986 gave small business a shot in the arm by taxing the first $50.000 of income at just 15% (the old law taxed income up to $25.000 at 15%). The maximum corporate tax rate has been slashed to 34% from 46% under the old law. That means more money in the corporate coffers for most small businesses.

The new tax law isn't a godsend for all businesses, however. Congress offset the loss of tax revenues from the cut in corporate tax rates by eliminating many tax credits and loopholes (such as the investment tax credit on capital expenditures) and by implementing changes in corporate accounting practices. The result is that manufacturing companies, transportation companies, real estate related businesses, and other concerns that have to make major capital purchases will pay more taxes than they would have under the old law.

All businesses will suffer from new rules on previously

deductible business expenses such as business meals and entertainment, purchase and use of company cars, deductions for home offices, expenditures for education, and corporate charitable contributions. Still fully deductible, however, are such perquisites as corporate travel, group life insurance and death benefits, medical and hospitalization insurance, disability income, and workman's compensation. The corporation can also still retain a substantial amount of profit to be invested with limited tax liability to the corporation (15%, the lowest rate) and none to the shareholders. The majority of small businesses—service, wholesale, or retail companies—will see profits rise under the new law.

The only problem for the shareholders (owners) of corporations is that when these profits are paid out as dividends, they're taxed twice—once as corporate profits, then as personal income of the recipient.

Subchapter-S Corporation. Tax experts unanimously agree that most small businesses derive the greatest financial benefits under the new tax law by electing to form Subchapter-S corporations. This type of organization provides the full protection from liability offered by other types of incorporation. But it allows its owners to avoid double taxation because all profits are taxed only once, as the personal income of the shareholders, just as if the corporation were a partnership. Any losses of the corporation are fully deductible from the gross personal income of the shareholders. Furthermore, the Subchapter-S corporation is excused from the stiff new corporate minimum tax under the new law, and is exempt from some of the costly accounting changes imposed on other forms of corporations.

The major disadvantages of electing a Subchapter-S corporation are that shareholders are limited to 35 people, none of the shareholders can be nonresident foreigners, and no shareholders can be corporations nor can the Subchapter-S corporation have corporate subsidiaries. The final disadvantage is that Subchapter-S status must be elected at the time the corporation is formed.

Before choosing any type of organization, you should thoroughly discuss your business plan with an attorney and an accountant who are experts in these matters. The organizational structure you choose must be broad enough to allow your company to do nearly everything—buy, sell, manufacture, own real estate, lease, borrow, loan, or whatever. Many companies start out in one business and end up in an entirely different one. You don't want to have to set up additional corporations or amend the bylaws of your present company to handle each new type of business or new business circumstance.

Raising the Capital

The second step in starting a small business, after the organization has been legally formed, is to capitalize it. This second step is by far more important and usually more difficult.

Financing is essential to any company. It is doubly important to a small business because its source of funds is usually so limited, whether for equity, working capital, or expansion. A major advantage of incorporation is that corporations can attract equity capital by issuing stock. It is difficult to finance a small business, but more difficult if it is not incorporated.

Yet one of the reasons often given as the major benefit of incorporation—the avoidance of personal liability—does not always hold for the small businesses. Unless a company has unusual assets, no bank or other lender—not even the Small Business Administration—will make a business loan unless the principals sign the note personally. This is true even though it is a corporation and may have reasonable assets. It is a fact of life. Face it. If you don't have confidence in your company, why should they?

How do you get the capital together to start a small business? The first place to look is right at home. Consider your own savings. Sell something. Mortgage or refinance your home. Borrow. From your relatives. From friends. But don't invest your own cash until you have exhausted all other avenues of funding. This is the rule of OPM, Other People's Money.

If you think you have a good idea for a business, investigate it thoroughly. Then gather sound statistics to project its possibilities. Assuming you can handle management or sales or some other role yourself, you may be able to put this intangible asset up as your share, with the money coming from other investors. This need not mean you will be an employee, either. For organizing the business, being the entrepreneur of the new company, you can be issued a percentage of the total authorized stock in payment for your efforts. Without putting up a dime.

If you are broke but want a business of your own—or at least one in which you are part-owner—don't waste any more time working for someone else. Get out and start organizing a business.

It may be easier to attract other investors, whether they be friends, relatives, or strangers, if you can also put in some cash. If you can, that reduces the amount needed from outsiders and increases your percentage of ownership. Maybe you have enough to capitalize the company alone. This is ideal in terms of ownership, though it has disadvantages, too.

The standard advice to entrepreneurs until the last decade was not only to use Other People's Money, but to borrow whenever possible. Double-digit interest rates in the early 1980s and the accompanying national credit squeeze made this advice suicidal. Although interest rates have subsequently fallen dramatically, today's risky economic climate means that recommendation is not only outdated but also dangerous.

Despite the drop in interest rates, the dramatic rise in

both bankruptcy filings and business failures that began in 1980 shows no signs of abating. From 1979 to 1984 the number of business bankruptcy filings jumped from 29,500 to 62,170, and the number of business failures soared from 7,564 to 31,334. A major reason is that small businesses are among the lower-rated borrowers, and always have to pay 2% to 8% more for bank loans than large corporations. With higher debt payments eating up working capital, thousands of businessmen find themselves on the road to insolvency.

The inescapable conclusion is that you should try to limit borrowings as much as possible. One sound alternative to direct investment of your money in the business is making a loan to the business. In this way you have provided needed capital, with interest payments to you and a business deduction (the interest) for the corporation.

When you do put in cash, as above, put in somewhat less than the company needs. The worst thing for a small, struggling company to have is plenty of cash. Consider the story of the electric pencil sharpener.

A former employee of mine inherited some money. In keeping with my philosophy he left to start a business of his own. Soon he called me, sounding very proud, anxious to show me his new offices. He had rented a building. In it he had put the newest and best machinery and equipment. The office chairs were of fancy leather and his desk was a beauty. "Look at this," he said expansively, "we even have an electric pencil sharpener." We sat down. He put his feet up on his fine new desk and asked me, "What do you think of my business?"

"What business?" I replied.

His company had not obtained its first order! Orders and production make a business, not desks and machinery. All he had was some hardware that might represent the potential of a business. He did not need all that machinery. He needed no fancy office equipment. He especially did not need an electric pencil sharpener because there were no orders to dull the pencil on! Worst of all, he had spent all his cash and left none for working capital.

There is one overriding consideration for not putting all your own cash into your business:

> *If the business is successful you will need your cash later to help it grow and expand. If it is not successful, you will have some cash left to start another business.*

Successful businessmen seldom operate with their own money if they can possibly avoid it. That is what capitalism is: a system in which professional business operations utilize other people's money for mutual gain.

Control

This brings up the question of whether you will control your new company, share control, or merely be a stockholder in a company controlled by others. Any of these situations is preferable to working for someone else. By the same token it is better to control your own business. Since it will probably be a corporation, this means that 51% of the stock must be yours or under your control. Assume your company will need $10.000 initial capital. Does this mean you must put up $5.100?

Definitely not. There need be no correlation between the capital paid in for stock and the working capital used by the company. A recently organized distributing company anticipates doing $200,000 in volume the first year. Paid-in capital? $2.500. The reason is simple. Why should funds sit idle, possibly subject to state corporation taxes? It is sounder to invest a minimum amount, then let the principals loan the new company money for working capital as needed.

For example, you organize your company with $3,000 initial paid-in capital. To assure control you put in $1,600 of this yourself, getting $1,400 from others, either investors or persons who will work with you in the new company and want a share in its ownership. Assuming a total of $10,000 is needed, this leaves $7,000 in operating capital to be raised.

First, see if you can secure "dating" (extended payment terms) from principal suppliers. If suppliers to whom you give $3,000 worth of business monthly allow you extended terms, this has the effect of adding $3,000 to your working capital. You may be able to make such an arrangement. Suppliers are often anxious to get the business of a new firm that appears to be well managed and to have a good chance of success. Also, they have you tied to them when they give dating, because they know you use the money freed by this arrangement for working capital. You will be in debt to them regularly and less apt to switch suppliers.

With $3,000 paid-in capital and $3,000 credit on dating, $4,000 would remain to be raised. You paid in some cash for your stock from your savings account of your life insurance, but they may have substantially more value left in them. Go to your bank. Put up your savings passbook or life insurance as collateral for a loan directly to the company. This has the added benefit of establishing the company's credit as it repays the loan. And you have not put very much of your cash directly into your business—in fact, only $1,600. Yet you control the company.

Many capable people simply do not have the capital to finance a business by themselves, and therefore the question of whether they are putting too much of their own money directly into the company is academic. If this is your position, don't despair. There are usually advantages in having to take others in with you. One is that it forces you to operate as a team and not as an individual. Two heads, or more, are better than one. No one ever got very big in the business world who could not delegate authority, confide in others and cultivate similar attributes of team management.

Where should you look for the persons who will become your teammates? This is almost entirely a question of the personalities involved. So-called silent partners are fine for some kinds of businesses. If the silent investor is a man with rich experience in the field you are going into, so much the better. But if he is just a guy with some extra cash who doesn't know much about business or your industry, watch out. Make him the last resort. Unless you get along well and candidly with your relatives or friends, ditto for them.

An objective approach to the operation of the business is what you are seeking. Maybe you will want to search out people with good backgrounds in business generally, or in your specific field, and try to get them to join you. You can run ads and attract working or silent investors that way. Many have done it. The business opportunities section of the want ads generally has several such ads. The point is that you need not be shy about asking people to join in your venture. There may be lots of them awaiting the opportunity. There are also as many ways to find them as there are types of companies to be started.

The matter of finding additional starting capital is almost entirely one of appealing to individuals. Banks cannot invest. Brokerage houses will not float a stock issue. The sources of all capital for small businesses are extremely limited. In his search for initial equity capital, the small businessman must look to individuals, mainly individuals like himself who want to be in business on their own.

Often the problem of taking someone else into the company does not come up until later. The owner has sufficient capital to get the operation under way, and only after growth pains set in is it necessary to look for new capital. The first thought of most individual owners (even though their concern may be a corporation) is to take in a "partner," another working executive who will buy stock. This is fine. But all too often it is handled in such a way that the person who started the company dilutes his interest far too much. When it comes time to take in more capital, his control becomes so diluted that it is lost.

This is simply bad planning. Instead of issuing treasury stock, that is, new shares that have not been issued before, sell the new shareholder some of your stock. Take the money yourself and put it into a money market mutual fund. Then when the company needs more capital, you can elect to fund it directly or extend a personal loan to the corporation.

How Much Money Do You Need?

The rule of thumb used by most venture capitalists and investment bankers is that a "start-up," or new business, needs enough capital to cover a full year's expenses without any income. Yes, yes. All new entrepreneurs insist their business will bring in a healthy amount of revenue within days or weeks or at least months of beginning operation. Forget all that for now. Pretend your fledgling concern will have absolutely no customers the first year. Absolutely none. Then compute reasonable expenses—rent, utilities, salaries, raw materials costs, production costs, supplies—the whole shebang for an entire year. That's the amount you should target as required capital.

To prove your case to bankers and potential investors, however, you'll have to develop a comprehensive business plan. This plan should include a brief statement concerning the type of business you will operate and its chief products within the context of a given industry and competition. You should describe the requirements of the business in terms of capitalization, plant and equipment, manpower, executives, distribution, marketing, promotion, and expectations of sales and expenses. The critical parts of the business plan are the so-called "pro formas"—the cash-flow projections and projected profit and loss statements for the first three to five years of operation. Keep in mind as you get out your calculator and ledger sheets that these figures must be within the realm of possibility.

In working out the projection, if you decide that 50 units of product X must be sold each month, the question is whether that number CAN be sold to the known market by a new company. If all this sounds complicated, be assured it can be. Hire an accountant to work through the pro forma statements with you. The money is well spent for accurate financial projections. The outcome of the projections may be a warning that you will have to lower your sights, at least initially. Or that you should avoid that business entirely.

A business of your own can be started with little or no capital of your own. Even if you have ten bucks you can buy a secondhand bike and start a paper delivery route. Many mail order businesses have been started with initial capital of $100. Believe it or not, manufacturing firms can be started for $500. Usually they are located in the basement, garage, or barn of the owner, and may have only one piece of machinery or use only hand tools. William Nickerson's best-seller tells in the title what can be accomplished with $1,000. *How I Turned $1,000 into $3 Million in Real Estate.* With $2,000, the sky could be the limit.

A word about when to take the plunge. Most of our creative ability is concentrated in the years before forty. We have more energy then, better health, and have had fewer disappointments and hard knocks. Take advantage of your youth. Don't work for GE or GM until your best years are past. Start now to work for yourself.

This is not to say one can't strike out on one's own later in life. Thousands have. If you are over 45 or 50 or even 60, no matter. But if you are a young person, ask yourself one question: Why should I wait to start in for myself?

CHAPTER III

Banks Then
and Now

ONCE initial capital has been invested, a small business is primarily dependent on banks for additional financing. Banks are the logical source for funds to increase working capital. But not the only source. (Tuck that away for future reference.)

Small business is usually local. Even a small manufacturer whose products are sold all over the country would have difficulty getting a loan from a bank in a distant city. He turns to his local lending source. This is fine—local banks should support local industry.

You would expect this common interest in the growth of a hometown to produce a good relationship between banks and their customers. Instead, it frequently results in just the opposite.

Why should this be? After all, most local banking volume originates with small business. In medium-sized and smaller cities, what are termed small businesses are, by comparison, the *big* companies of the locality. If there is a large company (or a branch of one) in a small town, it usually banks in a big city and only keeps a payroll ac-

count locally. Furthermore, most banks themselves fall
into the definition of small business. Thus banks should be
sensitive to the needs of their small-business neighbors—
but they seldom are.

To suggest an answer, we might look into some bank
history.

The Old-Time Banker

Many years ago, during the early growth period of our
nation, the banker was the most respected man in the
community. He was one of the town's more successful
men and usually the wealthiest. He obtained his wealth by
hard work and business risks in his earlier years. Later, in
his maturing years, he became head of a bank along with
his other holdings.

People looked up to this community leader. They respected him because of past success, his understanding of
financial matters, and unselfish devotion to the community. He usually contributed heavily to the local charities.
In the old days, bankers made their share of business
mistakes, but they profited by them, going on with courage
to make their personal fortunes and help others make
theirs. They provided employment, fostered ingenuity in
business, made a profit, reinvested, and made more profit.
This banker, and thousands like him, helped the country
grow and prosper. Small towns became large ones, larger
towns became small cities, and so on, helped by bankers
who were, above all, loyal to the town where they had
made their home and fortune.

People in the community came to the banker for *advice*
as well as money. He made loans based on his personal
business judgment along with his appraisal of the prospective borrower. He did not need a loan committee. He

knew the prospect, had confidence in him and his idea. When he made a loan he gave sound business advice with it—based on his personal experience in businesses other than banking. You depended on his advice, and hence your banker became an unofficial director of your company. If you got in trouble you went to your banker and worked it out together.

He was the Father Confessor, business-wise, of all local businessmen. He was very careful to keep your business problems to himself and never revealed a confidence. He never had to ask, "How's so-and-so's business doing?"

Compare this typical banker of old with those you know. Today's banker is not the wealthiest man in town. In fact, he seldom is considered part of the upper income group. His salary is adequate but not large. The main reason he has the job is usually because he values the security and prestige of being a bank officer. His personal business experience, outside of the bank, is usually nil. In your business, for example, what capacity could he fill? Your own salary is probably larger than his, or should be (not counting the fringe benefits you get by owning your own business). Could he be your purchasing agent? Engineer? Production manager? Sales manager? No, of course not! Chances are he is not fitted or trained for any job in your organization. How, then, is he fit to make a judgment about your company?

Your banker is part of a great bureaucracy: government regulations, red tape, Federal Reserve System, treasury bonds, loan committees, boards of directors, etcetera, etcetera. He is a semi-civil servant working in a secure job in a regulated, organized, socialistic system.

Certainly these people are necessary in our complicated business world. We have to have thousands upon thousands of government workers and bankers. Parkinson's

Law* says so. Fortunately (or unfortunately), there are enough of these people to fill the bill. They like security, pensions, fancy offices, titles. Do they have courage? Guts? Can they make decisions? Can they take, or make, a loan on a good business gamble? Are they equipped to help out when something goes wrong? What advice can they offer?

They just do not make many costly mistakes! They play it so close to the vest only a freak accident could cause one. When a company they have "helped" (usually with not enough money to do the job) "goes under" they have many outs. Personal endorsement by the owner, assignment of his life insurance, liens on the business equipment, chattels, accounts receivable, inventory, etcetera. Under the law they come ahead of other creditors. The poor vendor who has provided goods to the unfortunate firm must get in line. The bank comes first. Bankers have a soul-saving motto: "We can't throw good money after bad." This provides them with a wonderful *out* in case of trouble.

Bankers may indirectly put more companies in bankruptcy than anyone else. They say to themselves, "Let's put this guy out of his misery." What they mean is, "We're not capable of *helping* this guy out of his trouble with sound advice or know-how. Our board would criticize us for making further loans. And since we have plenty of security to protect us, let's close in while we still have it! We can't ever be found to have made a mistake."

Perhaps this is understandable. Around the turn of the century the average American lived on a farm. He was independent because he literally earned his livelihood with his two hands. As late as the Depression, Mr. Average American still lived in a small town. He didn't grow his

---

* Briefly, "Work expands as people become available."

own food any longer but he did have to earn his own way. He either owned or worked for a small local business. In both these stages of our national growth the banker financed nearly every venture. He was close to it and its entrepreneurs and employees. It was local. National brands and nationwide marketing were just developing. As an intelligent, well-respected businessman, who controlled the source of capital, the banker naturally got into profitable side businesses. He was then able to make banking decisions based on a knowledge of local business learned outside the bank.

Today the average American lives in a city, a suburb, or a region whose economic activity is tied to the nearest big city. These are large units with thousand of business enterprises there and thousands of national marketers selling into the area. Population is counted in millions. Complex government controls are needed. The banker's internal business has become so intricate that it takes special education plus years of on-the-job training to equip him. Any firsthand knowledge he acquires of other businesses is happenstance. Like all men faced with a totally bewildering environment, but with some education in one small phase of it, the banker tends to defend himself psychologically by pretending he really knows quite a bit about all business. After all, he can rationalize, isn't it the banks that make the whole system possible?

Though bankers undoubtedly favor free enterprise, what they mean is big business, or at least one bigger than your business is.

What to Expect from Your Bank

If you *don't* need money, banks will loan it to you.
Bankers talk about how they are risking their money on

you. To prove how small the bank's risk is, look at the money you were able to borrow in the past compared with the collateral they insisted on. Also ask them what *their* bad debt ratio is.

Forearmed by realizing your banker is not going out on a limb for you, you should examine bank methods and how they might be turned to your advantage or, at least, understand them.

BANKS ARE UNFAIR TO SMALL BUSINESS

1. Because of their position in the status quo, bankers often have a high-handed attitude toward those outside it. As independent molders of their own lives and futures, small businessmen fall far outside this status quo, where mass economic, social, and political power is the rule. Your philosophy and the banker's are usually opposite. Behind his sly probing may be one unstated question: Why can't you be more like the rest of us instead of going off on your own? He lives in a different world than you.

2. Banks, like all lenders, charge high, unrevealed interest rates whenever possible in spite of the Truth-in-Lending law. Like anyone else, they like to sell their product for the highest possible prices. Money is their product and interest is the price you pay, plus average balance in your checking account, service charges, etcetera. These prohibitive interest rates take their highest toll among small businessmen.

3. In order to continue a line of credit, or even extend new loans, banks like to see a small business showing a profit. There may be reasons why you should not show a profit. Perhaps you should be investing heavily in research to meet changing market conditions. Possibly you are tooling up for a new product. Often such expansion will be planned for a high profit year to reduce taxes. The banker is not interested. He wants you to show a profit because that has the appearance of success, if not the reality. This is a farce. Since he usually gets more than ample security for any loan, what difference should it make to the banker? Why should you show a profit just to have some of it go to the IRS?

4. When a small business has real need for money— perhaps because it had a rough year, or is growing faster than working capital can accrue through profits (after taxes)—the businessman exerts all his skill to get his bank to participate in his challenges and opportunities. Fearful of any risk, this is usually when the bank says no. Instead of forthrightly stating their reason, or even entering into a dialogue on the matter, you are simply told "the loan committee did not approve it." Or, a slight variation: "The bank examiners would criticize us if we made this loan."

5. In the last ten years our country's economy has grown 33%, but the number of commercial banks has grown a scant 2%. The reason is, of course, large banks gobbling up small banks through mergers and acquisitions. Small business needs small banks, yet there are fewer and fewer every year.

BANKS HELP SMALL BUSINESSES STAY SMALL

1. Because of their fear of risk, banks invariably require collateral or security considerably in excess of loans. For the small business this has the effect of it never getting quite the amount of money it needs. It is a standard pro-

cedure with banks to loan small business just a little less than its requirements. They consider this a technique for protecting themselves, for making the loans "safer." Actually, the opposite is true. By loaning less than is needed, banks force small business to stay small. To cut back plans. To postpone essential action because it cannot be funded. Banks would be better protected if their small business customers had sufficient funds so they could grow bigger and financially sounder. What would society think of a physician who gave not quite enough medicine to his patients? This would make sense only for a doctor in cahoots with the undertaker. Bankers are interested first in protecting themselves, whatever the effect on their customers. This is frequently covered up by asking their customer, "Are you sure this [amount] is enough?" This can throw you off guard when requesting a loan.

2. When a small business does get a slightly-less-than-the-amount-required loan, chances are it will be on a short-term basis. Accountants consider loans for less than a year as current, above "the line." A three-year commercial loan is maximum at most banks. Even then, one-third of it is "above the line" in current liabilities. The borrower is constantly scraping up all loose funds and any profits after taxes to repay the bank. The loan has had the effect of bailing him out of a tight spot or enabling the first step in an expansion program. Then progress stops while all available funds are rechanneled to repay the bank. Growth depends on having borrowed funds long enough to concentrate on utilizing them effectively. Even when you have reduced the loan substantially, the banker usually retains all the collateral you gave him originally.

3. Banks practice extensive "cooperation among lenders." First, there is a thorough exchange of credit informa-

tion on *you* and your company. Much of this so-called factual data is *opinion*. Because bankers are trained to think negatively, this opinion is mostly negative.

I don't mean to imply some grand conspiracy. The bankers don't sit down together and work out a strategy. At least, I don't *think* they do. Yet it has the same effect. They even have a special language among themselves, full of cozy innuendoes, that have very subtle meanings within their fraternity.

Don't get the impression banks don't want to loan money. In recent years the fact that they *must* make loans to make a profit has been openly discussed—and even advertised. They are all fighting for the larger, successful companies. None of them want the newer, riskier businesses.

Bankers discuss loan situations among themselves in a way that would make the Federal Trade Commission blush. That is why it is difficult to change banks once you become a borrower. With financial difficulties it's tough to change due to your problems. If successful, it would be unfair to leave the bank that *helped you* without extenuating circumstances. A legitimate reason for change is when you outgrow the small bank and need a larger institution.

This is why it sometimes seems that when you have told your story to one banker, you have told it to them all. Most bankers and lenders are in collusion, but it is not fraudulent. In any other busniess it would be price-fixing and restraint of trade, and the government would be busy policing it. Through the Federal Reserve system, banks do it *with* government help. Wouldn't it be nice if your company could do a little price-fixing aided and abetted by the U. S. government?

BANKS FORCE SMALL BUSINESSES INTO REGRETFUL
SITUATIONS TO PROTECT THEMSELVES

1. In their desire to avoid taking a fair risk of a local business enterprise, banks have forced many companies to take steps which proved harmful. A frequent example is mergers which do not pan out, or do not benefit the local or national economy. These are brought about because the bank gets panicky and wants to improve its position by placing the debtor into the cushier assets of another company. The results for the parties to the merger may be dubious. The bank's protective collateral always seems to increase. Most of the conglomerates have recently proven that any bank encouragement to merge was wrong.

2. If a borrower experiences hard times, another way out for the bank is to put a partner into the situation who has cash. "You need more equity," they will say. "Maybe I know someone . . . " The new partner usually buys in at an extremely good price. The small businessman is given the alternative of being bankrupted by having his note called, so there is little he can do. When criminals use such tactics they are called nasty names. In a very real sense, when a banker suggests a partner he is making an offer you cannot refuse.

3. When a small business seems to be making the grade, perhaps growing toward becoming big business, bankers are equally ready to *help*. They sense a new arrival in the circle of successful companies to whom they want to loan money. Naturally, they *want* to speed you into that charmed group. A rapid way to accomplish this is by having your company go public. The stock issue will increase the capitalization, but the expansion necessary to keep shareholders happy will have you back at the loan officer's

desk shortly. The net result will be that you have lost some or all control. The bank now has a borrower with an established price for its stock, thus providing itself with extensive additional protection. If trouble should occur despite this, a publicly held concern is much simpler to overhaul, to force into management and policy changes, than a possibly recalcitrant owner.

Your banker's suggestions to help you grow, or to get you out of trouble, must be accepted. But with a grain of salt. He has something to lose—or gain—and can hardly be considered objective.

Bankers may disagree with these interpretations. The writer admits knowing little about the banking business per se, except what he has learned from being on the other side of the desk and its actual effect on small business.

The purpose here is not to attack banks or bankers but to help small businessmen. This merely outlines the problem by giving a small businessman's view of bankers. The key is to find out what you might do about it.

CHAPTER IV

If Bankers Are Friends, Who Needs Enemies?

In the past, banks were wary of making loans to small businesses and threw up obstacles in the credit path of entrepreneurs. While it is still not *Easy* to wrest credit from the vise-like grip of a loan officer, more and more small companies are finding a warm reception at their local bank. Many banks have developed small business account officers specializing in the particular credit and servicing needs of these companies and are creating special cash management and electronics services for them. Also, there is a growing trend toward narrowing the premium small businesses pay on their loans and to extending longer-term loans—up to five years in some areas—rather than limiting credit access to short-term rollover debt.

How to Borrow From Your Banker

Still, there is a perceived reluctance on the part of loan officers to make loans to small companies. To help win favorable treatment from your bank, financial experts say the best insurance is solid advance work. Prepare. Yourself. Your business plan. Your financial statements. Your accountant. And your spiel. Bankers say that fewer than 10%

of prospective borrowers appear at the bank adequately prepared. That makes it very easy for them to say no.

If you want to improve your chances at the loan window, try the following.

Seek out a bank that specializes in or is at least interested in nurturing small business accounts. If you head right for the biggest bank in the city that caters to Fortune 500 corporations, you may find yourself with a "no" before you even open your mouth.

And once you've blundered into the wrong type of bank, you've made it even harder for yourself to get a loan from your second choice. Why? Because all banks file their credit applications and disposition results with regional and national credit reporting bureaus. And both the fact of your application and that "no" will be reported to a bureau. So when you go in the door to Bank No. 2, the second loan officer will query the credit bureau and discover that you've already been rejected by Bank No. 1. There is a very good chance that Bank No. 2 will think that Bank No. 1 rejected you for cause—that they found out something about your company that you haven't told them, perhaps—and Bank No. 2 will play it safe and say "no," too.

When you go to the bank you have chosen, take along with you a complete and accurate business plan plus cash flow projections and pro forma balance sheets prepared by a professional accountant. You might also take along a personal balance sheet—and the accountant, if he'll come. Bankers like to ask questions and they like to ask them of financial whizzes, in jargon, if at all possible. Anytime you want to reassure a banker, bring in an accountant to converse with him. Some bankers say having an accountant appear with you can improve your chance of a loan approval by 75%.

Another excellent reason for playing the banker two-on-one is that the accountant can probably make an excellent case for the right kind of financing—with a maturity on the loan that your business can support. Too short a loan period can force you into depleting your working capital and bring you back to the bank for refinancing, which will mean higher interest rates and a squeeze on your profitability.

Don't inflate your needs. Ask for a reasonable amount on your loan but not much more. Banks don't like to lend extra money. And if you have specific targets for the loan money—like $10,000 for a piece of equipment and $5,000 for working capital—spell that out. The bank may want to break that out into two separate transactions, say a five-year loan for the equipment and a line of credit for the $5,-000. Bankers get very suspicious of numbers that don't add up and figures that seem inflated. If you want a yes to your request, don't play games.

Be prepared to demonstrate to the bank that you're a solid citizen of good character. Sometimes banks—especially in small communities—will bend a little for someone who's active in civic affairs and goes to church on Sunday. Don't lie, just spiff up your track record.

Keep in mind that this is a sales call just like those you make on behalf of your company. You're selling the banker on yourself, your prospects, and the management of your company. That means you should be able to carry on an intelligent conversation with the banker and demonstrate that you have a solid understanding of the economy, business in general, the industry in which you are operating, and the competition. Don't appear so parochial that the loan officer is concerned about your awareness of the business climate in which you must make decisions.

Make an appointment. Don't just show up. Bankers are busy, too. And even if they're not, they like to feel like they're in control. Unexpected supplicants make them nervous. Besides, they'd like to get as much respect as a physician, dentist, or attorney. And all those folks require appointments. Besides, if you ask for an appointment you're demonstrating professionalism and business savvy. That should help your image with The Man (or Woman).

Be Prepared—In Writing

Get together all the facts about your business. Don't try to hide anything. If this is a formal request for a loan and not an exploratory visit, bring all the facts with you. This statement should show why you need the funds, the status of your business, and how you can repay the loan. This means you should have:

1. Recent balance sheet.
2. Recent profit and loss statement.
3. Company brochure, facilities booklet, or written statement about what your firm does.
4. Product literature, if a manufacturer, wholesaler, or retailer.
5. Written statement telling why the money is needed.
6. Written statement telling how you are doing in relation to your competitors.
7. Written outline of your plans for the future.
8. Projections of sales and profits for six months or a year ahead (pro forma statement).
9. Personal financial statement (for yourself *and* any other major owners) listing all assets and liabilities outside the business. This should include your home

real estate, interest in other businesses, savings accounts, automobiles and other personal property, bank loans, life insurance and its cash value.

10. Previous year's financial statements.

11. If you have received major contracts or orders, have been the subject of publicity articles, or have any other pertinent statistical or printed data (e.g., the number of active customers), bring it along with you.

12. Research summaries—especially market and product research—make excellent exhibits in your case for a loan.

If some of this material reveals you are having problems, or recently had some, bring it regardless. Do not try to hide this. Bankers have an informational network that would do credit to the CIA. They will find it out anyway. If you tell him first you can plausibly explain it. The commercial loan officer is an employee only. He cannot make a decision. He will not trust you if you do not provide him with all the facts, on paper, for his files.

If yours is a new business and most of the material deals in futures—don't be discouraged. Enter the bank even more proudly, like a new father passing out cigars. Every town needs new businesses. *You* are the brave, confident, hard-working citizen who has taken personal risk to enhance the community.

Whatever you do, don't make any of these exhibits contingent on getting the loan. For instance, in your forecast of the future don't say, "If our company can borrow $X, then we will be able to do so-and-so." This may sound sensible but it isn't. It puts you squarely in the hands of the banker, as if he were deciding your fate. Take the victorious attitude instead. Assume you will get the loan from one source or another. Make your projections positive statements which announce that you are going to do such-and-such (whether you do it through *him* or someone else). You are doing him the favor of offering his bank your business.

Dialogue Between Banker and Borrower

Deal with the highest-ranking officer you possibly can preferably the president. At least the vice-president in charge of the commercial loan department.

If it is necessary to wait a few days for an appointment with the president, wait. This shows you are in no rush and not in trouble, or the victim of poor planning. You can usually get an appointment with a lower officer by walking in. What good can he do for you before the loan committee? Timing is one of the weapons in business dealings, as you have probably learned only too well. Banks will use it on you. So, use it on them.

When you first sit down in the luxurious leather chair, and after the phony pleasantries of the day are dispensed with, *watch out!* You are about to be trapped. The banker will say (as he quickly glances over your statement, pretending to drink it all in, but actually comprehending little), "How much money do you want?" His voice is so benign and he seems like such a nice guy that you unhesitatingly mention an amount. If you do, you have just *lost the first round.*

You and your accountants have probably been wrestling with what amount is needed for weeks. It wasn't an arbitrary decision. Nor was the figure easily arrived at. Yet you tossed it off to the banker as if it were both. You have now innocently provided him with the exact location and description of his adversary. Once you reveal it, he can attack it.

"Why do you need it?" "How do you know this is enough?" "How do you know this isn't too much?" "How long do you need it for?" "Why can't you get along without it?" He may trap you still further by emphasizing his question, "Are you sure this is enough?" If you answer yes, he has really got you.

He has saved himself hours of agonizing labor in the process. Bankers are both busy and lazy (banker's hours and all that). All he has to prove now is why you either need more or shouldn't have the amount you requested. This is easy. Anyone with a smattering of business experience can rip any small business statement to shreds. Bankers sure can do this, and he is very safe in doing so because you would not be there if you didn't need money. Much about a business is not, cannot be, reflected in its financial statement. That is why you should take along pertinent material which goes beyond your financial statements.

The I-Don't-Know Method

What you should have said, when the banker asked how much you wanted to borrow, is, "I don't know." And quickly added, "But I thought you, as my banker, could help us determine this."

This avoids all the pat questions the banker is so carefully trained to ask. He not only has to study your statements but *must* get to know something about your business. He should anyway, of course. It is amazing how little most bankers do know about their customers' businesses.

He knows he can't insult a customer by saying, "Your business isn't worthy of any loan." That is seldom the problem. The real questions are: How much? For how long? At what rate? How will it be repaid? Now *he* must discover how much your company is entitled to borrow. You won the first round by *not* answering his direct question.

You have now put your banker to work for you. Strengths or weaknesses he discovers will be pointed out to you. Policies you can improve will be questioned and suggestions made. By having him pore over your statements and material, you may learn something which only an objective outsider would catch.

More important, from now on you and your banker are negotiating *not* on whether he will make a loan, but on the amount. While he strives to evaluate your company scientifically, you will have the opportunity to show him things he otherwise would not know. To make the most of this, invite him to your plant or place of business. This will allow you more time to do a selling job. Now he is the stranger on *your* home ground. Fill his head and his file with all sorts of reasons why the bank should make the loan. Show him what an assest you are, or can be, to the community. Tell him, as if letting him in on a highly guarded secret, of your great plans for the future.

This technique is important even after you have a long-standing relationship with the bank and arrange loans by phone. When the banker on the other end of the line asks, "How much do you want to borrow this time?" say, "C'mon over and see what you think." Then sell, sell, sell when he gets there. Subtly, of course.

Under any circumstances, whether at your plant or his

desk in the bank, do not tell him how much you want. At least not until you have done all the selling, forecasting, and convincing you can. Try to force *him* to bring the matter to a head.

If you have done all you can and he still has not mentioned any figure, you might try one or two on for size. By now you know him better and he is more familiar with your business. When you mention a figure, watch his face and especially his eyes. You might say, "Do you think we need as much as eighteen or twenty thousand?"

Actually you want $15,000, but you have got to make him a hero. He became a banker because he likes the prestige of working in the most imposing building in town. If he had the ability to be an aggressive businessman, facing competition, taking risks, working long hours, meeting payrolls, fending off creditors and collecting from accounts, he would be your competitor, not your banker. Or, if all your competition had his personality traits you would own the bank and be hiring him to work there for you.

The world is full of little demigods like your banker, and they must be treated so. Make him a hero. Mention a figure larger than you are after and let him act out his part by cutting it. He will probably cut down whatever figure you give, so if you mention the accurate one you will wind up with less than you need.

If you have been master of the interview, he will say, "I think I might be able to convince our loan committee that you should have twelve thousand five hundred." You look hurt and counter by saying, "You are probably right, but do you think they would consider fifteen?" Follow this up with one last sales point that you have been saving for dessert, adding quickly, "After all, our checking account balance for the past eight months has averaged twenty-eight hundred dollars."

This average—called a compensating balance—may affect the amount you can borrow. For example. if your average balance for the past year is $1,000 and the bank uses a 20% formula. you might be considered sound for a $5,000 loan. In giving your average balance. which is another exhibit you might take to the initial loan conference. pick the number of months that are the most favorable to you. If. for the past four months. the average balance was $1,500. but for the past year only $900, present the four-month figure even though it is a shorter period.

Figuring your average balance is easy. Take your bank statement and add the daily balances together. Then divide by the number of days. Include your payroll account also.

Banks use deposits to your checking account as part of their vital cash flow. yet they pay you little or nothing for it. In fact. many banks not only pay no interest on checking accounts. but also add on service charges. It pays to shop for the best deal in business checking, but you'll never find a bank that pays you as much to use your money as you pay to use theirs. It is not good strategy to mention this directly. You might make a casual remark or a joke of it, just to remind your banker of the fact.

Getting the banker to visit your place is key to the I-Don't-Know method. If he turns you down without a visit, he has made an irresponsible decision. From bank management's viewpoint. the same is true in reverse. He acts irresponsibly if he approves a loan without seeing your operation.

To help you follow your banker's conversation, the following is a primer to the twelve most common loan categories used by commercial banks. This banker's dozen falls into three broad areas: short-term, medium-term, and long-term maturities.

Short-Term Loans

This refers to debt that matures in less than a year. In practice, however, many banks include loans of two to three years' maturity here. Small businesses usually obtain short-term debt to finance inventory or receivables, especially if their companies handle seasonal or perishable products. The five types of short-term debt are as follows.

1. *Line of Credit.* This is a specific sum granted to a company for its use as needed. Sometimes a line of credit is extended for just 30 days, sometimes for two years, with repayment tied to anticipated revenues. The interest on a credit line is computed only on the amount actually used. Commitment fees of one half to one percent of the total credit line are charged for reserving the funds. Some banks waive this fee if the company maintains a compensating balance—an amount that must be held on deposit with the bank throughout the loan period. Short-term lines of credit must be paid up periodically at most banks, with the general rule that the line must be cleaned up for 30 days a year. Revolving lines of credit, however, require annual review and renewal, but do not have to be paid off completely. As the funds are drawn the line diminishes, but as it is repaid, the line expands.

2. *Inventory Loan.* These short-term loans require collateral—usually the inventory that they are to be used to

buy. Repayment is made as the inventory is sold and receivables paid up. These loans usually run six to nine months.

3. *Commercial or Time Loan*. This type of debt is a straightforward lump sum loan made by the bank and repaid in a lump sum at the end of its term, usually three to six months.

4. *Accounts Receivable Financing*. Banks will usually advance 65% to 80% of the face value of past-due accounts (usually on accounts that are less than 60 days past due and which are credit worthy). The debt is repayable as the customers pay up the accounts. Usually you, as the borrower, must endorse the customers' checks over to the bank as they come in; the bank then takes out its portion and deposits the balance in your account. Interest is charged only on the outstanding accounts receivable financed.

5. *Factoring*. This is one of the oldest methods of commercial financing. It is common in the garment industry and has spread to other industries, including electronics and appliances. Simply put, it is a variation on accounts receivable financing. It is also the most costly form of short-term debt. The bank or factor simply buys receivables outright from the borrower, at a large discount of course, assuming the credit risk and making the collections.

Medium-Term Loans

These loans usually range from one to five years in length and are used to finance expansion or purchases of machinery and equipment, furniture and fixtures. Banks usually require additional collateral for loans of these maturities and may also impose restrictions on the company's operations, by requiring maintenance of a certain level of working capital, or ratio of current assets to current liabilities. Two types of medium-term loans are the term loan and the monthly payment business loan.

Term Loan. Such debts usually provide 80% to 90% of the total cost of the project or equipment, and either run for the useful life of the asset involved or are written for five years with a refinancing clause. Repayment usually is structured in quarterly installments of principal plus interest, with the interest declining over the term of the loan.

Monthly Payment Business Loan. This is similar to a term loan but the payments are divided into equal monthly installments.

Long-Term Loans

Loans of five or more years are the hardest to obtain and are usually granted only for such major projects as the purchase of real estate or a major plant expansion or acquisition.

Commercial and Industrial Mortgages. These are usually extended when a company wants to buy the building that it has been renting. Such mortgages usually cover 75% of the appraised value of the property.

Real Estate Loan. These refer to second mortgages and wraparound mortgages granted by banks on real estate already owned by the corporation.

Personal Loan. These are loans based on the assets of the owner of the corporation. The assets most commonly put up as collateral are marketable securities, certificates of deposit, money market mutual fund accounts, savings accounts, or real property.

Asset-Based Loan. This type of loan is usually used only when a company wants to take over another company, using the assets of the target concern to finance the purchase. This is called a leveraged buyout. Banks may grant a loan for as much as 70% of the purchase price, using as collateral receivables, raw materials, inventory, equipment, and machinery; banks usually charge two to three percentage points over the prime lending rate on these loans.

Startup Loan. Existing companies that want to start new companies may obtain a term loan from a bank's venture capital division with a Small Business Administration guarantee if they also put significant amounts of their own money and personal assets of the owners into the deal.

What Banks Can Give Besides Loans

You should not resent your banker's questions. See what you can learn from them. If he asks why your accounts receivable are high and you explain that the figure is normal for your business, follow through by inquiring what data he may have on new collection techniques. Or ask what your competition and other companies are doing, and how. He talks with businessmen all day long. His bank is the clearinghouse for gossip, and he also has legitimate inside information which may be helpful to you. Turn his inquisition into an educational session. Don't be disappointed if you cannot learn much at any specific session. Keep trying. Your positive, willing-to-learn attitude should impress him.

Major banking institutions and the Federal Reserve system have tremendous research departments. Some of the nation's basic economic statistics originate there. You have access to this storehouse simply by asking. Even if your bank is a small one, it has a relationship of one kind or another with the banks doing this research, and can get it for you. Make your banker your research director. You are paying him anyway, so you might as well.

When he secures statistics and other data for you, natural curiosity will see to it that he looks over the material—and becomes better educated about your business. Knowing you keep an active interest in research is bound to make an impression.

Sooner or later your banker will ask to see a cash flow chart on your business. If you do not have a controller, or treasurer, make a rough draft yourself. Sit down with your banker and let him *help you* fill in the detail.

Robert Morris Associates' annual *Statement Studies* is an example of the extent of cooperation among bankers. But it can help the small businessman by providing general guidelines so he can see how he is doing. Your banker will consult the *Studies*, or similar factual data shared among banks, when he evaluates your company for a loan. Beat him at this game by asking to borrow a copy and using his own statistics in your presentation. Or, buy a copy. Your banker can tell you where to order.

As an information source your banker can be invaluable. And free. This is the one thing he can give you beside loans and headaches.

Who Decides Yes or No?

When you have made the best possible loan presentation, and you are dying to know your banker's answer, all he usually says is, "I'll take this up with our loan committee." You have spent long hours on this. You are sure of all your figures. Your accountant has stayed after hours working with you. Production and sales departments worked overtime to help with the forecasting. Now you want an answer.

As you gather up your papers it occurs to you that the banker may already have made up his mind. Maybe this loan committee bit is just a stall. Or, perhaps he will present it to them but in a negative way. This worries and frustrates you. It dawns on you that even if he is in favor of the loan he cannot possibly make as good a presentation to the committee as you could. You mull this over. Take into consideration, you warn yourself, that though your company is small, his income is less than yours. He hasn't got your capital gains opportunities. And he has to answer to a string of directors, while you are independent. Can he be anxious to see you build an even more successful company?

You decide to take the matter into your own hands. "Who are the members of the loan committee?" you ask politely.

"It is a policy of the bank not to reveal this," the banker replies, proving he is a front man. Half-joking he adds, "Maybe you wouldn't want to know."

Now you *are* frightened. Is the uncle of one of your ex-employees on the committee? Or the bank director whose wife misunderstood that remark your wife made at the Woman's Club luncheon? If only you could go before the committee yourself!

In desperation, as you turn to go, you say, "Would it be possible for me to present our case to the committee?"

Forget about the loan, friend. You just blew it. You might as well have told your banker you have no confidence in him, even as an errand boy, to carry your loan application to the men who really decide yes or no. He certainly will not try to sell your loan to them now. You, in your impatience and frustration, have made the decision on your loan yourself.

There is no end to the patience you must have with bankers. After waiting to get an appointment with the president, after months spent deciding what amount you need, after weeks preparing the loan presentation, after a long session or two of inquisition at the bank—after all this your patience gave out a minute too early. The major weapon of your adversary, the banker, is unlimited patience. Time is on his side. You must learn to out-wait him. Realizing this before you take the first step may be the most important consideration in borrowing money.

Timewise, he has all the advantage. By planning ahead, you too can play his waiting game. This will make a point with your banker, since he knows only capable executives in well-managed companies can be so relaxed. Don't wait until you need the money tomorrow. Tell him you are going to need it within the next month or two.

Bankers will use the "loan committee" line for every situation where they want to gain time or turn you down. It nicely shifts blame to an anonymous group and away from the officer with whom you negotiated. It leaves the door open for you to give them your business in the future. They will not loan to you now when you are struggling. But when you have become successful, they don't want you to feel alienated. It is part of the banker's pattern of taking no risk. He will not risk offending you, since it might cost him business some day.

Two can play at that game. To field tricky questions, or gain time, tell him you will have to take it up with your "Board of Directors," "Executive Committee," "Advisors," or "Accountant." You may really have to do this. This is the way the game is played, and unless you have this tool in your kit you are disadvantaged. Of course, you had better let your "Board" in on what you are doing in case the banker asks them.

If you want to ask some questions, even embarrassing ones, attribute them to your Board of Directors. "My Board wanted me to ask why you are charging twelve percent interest when Bigtown Bank's new going rate is nine percent." Under this guise all manner of things are possible which could not otherwise be accomplished without setting up a confrontation with your banker.

At last your loan application is ready to be acted on. The loan committee is meeting Tuesday. You need the money to stay competitive, and it has you worried. You don't get much sleep over the weekend. Monday keeps you busy with its usual first-of-the-week problems. Tuesday morning you attend a sales meeting followed by lunch with a major customer. By the time you get back to the office Tuesday afternoon you can't stand the suspense any longer. So you call the bank.

"Mr. Friendly, this is Woodby Borrower. I was wondering how my loan was coming."

"Well, funny you called. I was just going to call you."

He wasn't, of course, because he shies away from these moments of truth and knew you would call anyway.

"Yes? . . ." Your voice dies away in anticipation.

"I'm afraid I've got an unhappy report for you," he begins, to let you down easily. You know you have had it.

Bankers never come right out and say, "I decided your company isn't worthy of a loan." They are better psychologists than that. They sugar-coat the bitter pill. You feel like you have been KO'd, but you have got to keep on your feet and swinging.

There is always the possibility the answer to your loan request will be no. Face it in advance, so if you are turned down you will still have a positive program. Usually the bad news comes gift-wrapped and insulated. "I brought up your case before our loan committee," the banker recites, "and tried my best to convince them to make this loan. They voted on it and turned it down." You wonder why and ask. The usual stock answers are so phony the bank might as well mimeograph a sheet of them then check off the one being used that week. Among these excuses are:

"You need more equity capital in your business."

"We have too many loans out like this now."

"The bank examiners are coming."

"The savings department has had heavy withdrawals." Getting the real reason why the bank refused your loan is difficult. The information would be extremely helpful to you. It might point out a defect or weakness in your company. It might avoid problems that the bank sees building up in your industry. It would surely help you get a loan somewhere else. That is a major reason you cannot get the truth.

Your bank may not wish to loan you their money—but they want yours. So much so that they employ the tactic of not telling you all they know about you. Their search for the truth of your figures took place mainly behind your back. You are asking them to their faces.

They do not want to make a loan—but neither do they want to lose your personal savings and checking accounts, your company checking and payroll accounts, your wife's Christmas Club, and other accounts which contribute to their essential cash flow. And when you finally make it big, then they will want your loan business. Although they spend lots of front money, free gifts, etcetera, to give the appearance, banks simply have not learned that honesty and forthrightness are the best policy. Their methods might sometimes be called "financial malpractice."

The reason bankers get away with this is *our* fault. They take advantage of our natural desire to hide the fact that we were *turned down*. They do everything they can to soften the *no*. Once they have finally come out with it, using whatever phraseology they can concoct to avoid the simple two-letter word, they expect the matter to disappear in silence. They are not going to mention it—except to the Credit Bureau and other portions of their CIA underground—and feel confident you will be too embarrassed to do so. That is why . . .

The best thing you can do, if your bank refuses you a loan, is to broadcast the fact all over town.

Don't run away. You have nothing to hide. It happens to General Electric also. It is the bank which must defend its decision before public opinion when you confidently spread the word that they denied your request. People will assume the turndown was unjustified or you would not be talking about it! It would be helpful to small business everywhere if, whenever a loan is refused, the applicant gave it widespread publicity.

Publicizing the turndown puts pressure on the bank. Other small businessmen may feel the banker is not favorable to small business and look elsewhere for their banking. Banks need small business. They could not survive without them. Their image can be severely damaged if it becomes known they are not serving small business.

When your company becomes successful, do not forget which bank refused to help you. Too often businessmen run back to the same one, giving bankers the impression they can turn down anyone with impunity. When you are more successful do not forget to remind everyone that Ultraconservative National turned you down. Your success proves they were wrong.

After you have been turned down don't hesitate to go immediately to another bank and start over. Banks are, *or should be*, competitors. Tell the new bank you were turned down and the reasons given you. He will chalk up a point for your frankness.

Start all over again.

CHAPTER V

Other Money-Lenders

THERE are other money sources than banks for small business. The most important, the Small Business Administration, came into being precisely because banks were not doing their jobs. Though SBA loans are sometimes shared with a local bank, they exist because the Federal government formally realized that small business was being financially undernourished by private money sources. Even factoring houses have shown an increasing interest in small business in recent years. This stems from recognition of the size and potential of the market—and the scarceness of other money sources for small business.

Basically, all money lenders are alike. *Wise borrowers treat them alike.* Rules previously discussed for doing business with banks apply equally to other money sources. Except for SBA, the money lender's motive is to make a profit—which is as it should be. SBA makes no "profit" but it expects the economy and the community to benefit from its loans.

If you possibly can, set up competition between your sources. Let them know that, like everyone else in business, they might have to meet someone else's price. You undoubtedly have more than one source for other purchasing. Let the same rule apply in financing.

While you are struggling to get established, this may not be possible. The wisest course may be to stick with the financing which is helping you.

Many small businessmen are unaware of alternate money sources. Because banks are the traditional financiers, a myth has been built up around them. Part of it is that banks are always the best place to borrow, and that loans from any other source are more expensive and a sign of trouble. It is necessary for us to delve into this myth and explode it. A few pointers on alternative money sources may help.

Trade Credit as a Source of Financing

Before any borrowing, the smart businessman makes sure his present capital is getting maximum use. Many small businessmen do not take full advantage of available credit. Some seem afraid to ask for dating on billing and other concessions from their suppliers. Others hesitate to incur debt because they worry about possible inability to repay.

The small businessman who worries about incurring debt will remain small. The ones who really grow will incur heavy debt. Trade credit accounts for a major part of the working capital of business today. If credit were not available, imagine how much more cash your company would need.

Small Business Administration

To speak of other money sources for small businesses is to speak primarily of the Small Business Administration. No other compares with it in size or significance, concern or effectiveness.

So much has been written by and about SBA that most small businessmen are familiar with its loan facilities. If not, they should be. Recitation of facts about this Federal agency is unnecessary here. Your nearest SBA office can bring you up to date. Their policies frequently change with politics.

SBA's loan policies show why it is a boon to small business. Earning power is often more important than collateral in the granting of its loans. It may take a second mortgage. There is no interference in clients' business unless financial records show deterioration. Then it comes in only to find the trouble and actually help you straighten it out.

Some SBA loans may be for as long as ten years. Working capital loans can be for four to six. This is in stark contrast to the prohibitive short-term loans peddled by banks. On direct loans, or SBA's portion of loans in which it participates with a bank, interest is very reasonable. Again, a far cry from the sometimes detrimental rates charged by banks.

SBA exists solely to aid small business. By its nature, this Federal agency is committed to doing everything possible to help its clients succeed. These are the kind of lending policies small business has long needed.

The problem, in the minds of most small businessmen, is that banks have created the wrong impression of SBA. They will tell you it is a last resort. That you must be in real trouble before SBA will help. That it is government interference. That SBA will tell you how to run your business.

This defamation campaign by banks is untrue and unfair. Many small businessmen have been frightened away by such propaganda. Companies which could be helped by SBA have been wary of applying. The fact is there would be no SBA if the banks, over the years, had been performing the service they should have. They brought the SBA on themselves.

Your *friendly banker*, unwilling to provide you with a long-term loan, may suggest SBA as a "last resort." He wants you to feel that your business is so badly off he cannot help you. "There is one last resort," he says, as if recommending an undertaker. But SBA may be your best bet.

Certainly the monthly drain on your earnings is less with a six-year SBA loan than with a bank loan which must be repaid in three. And think how much better it is to borrow from a source that will send experts to help you overcome your problems. SBA is committed to doing everything possible to help you succeed. Failure of a client is a black eye to SBA. To a bank it is merely a collection procedure of your collateral.

SBA's method of financing small business shows how the bankers influenced the law which established it. It appears it was not set up only to help the small businessman but also the banks. Consider the benefits banks derive. First, the funds legally available for them to loan are substantially increased. Second, the necessity of taking risk on small business is shifted to the government. Third, small businesses can become prosperous and thus good bank customers at public risk and expense. Fourth, the stigma of denying financial assistance to a community's small business is partially removed.

Ironically, the bankers, who are usually conservative, have fostered this somewhat socialistic Federal agency.

During high interest rates, of course, banks are reluctant to have another government agency looking over their shoulder. A participating loan with the SBA gives them less freedom, and they would prefer to remain independent.

Nevertheless, banks do participate with the SBA, and in recent years 90% of the Small Business Administrations' transactions have been loan guarantees. The SBA will guarantee between 50% and 80% of loans under three programs: the 7A Term Loan Guarantee, the Economic Opportunity Loan, and the Operation Business Mainsteam loan. The SBA will also guarantee up to 90% of a line of credit secured against actual contracts held by a small business.

Direct loans by the SBA are limited to $100,000. They're only available when an SBA guarantee has been rejected by two banks and when very limited funds are available.

Even loan guarantees are not available if a business can obtain funds from a bank or other equity sources without SBA assistance. Ostensibly this is to preclude government from competing with private enterprise, a theory most businessmen favor. Practically, it fosters and sanctions the restraint of trade that exists in the banking industry.

In other words, the guarantees are not to small business, but to the banks! Your risk is undiminished, but the bank is protected.

One point SBA's loan program has proven is that liberal loans to small businesses are not risky, as banks insist. Of $725 million outstanding in SBA loans at the beginning of fiscal 1966, less than $5 million was in guaranteed loans. That is, this tiny percentage had actually been taken over from the banks by SBA because of borrower default. SBA was committed to purchase an additional $135 million. That is, they guaranteed this amount and will purchase it in case of default. So sound are these loans, however, that on SBA's books $115 million of the $135 million has been written off as "reduction for estimated loans not requiring purchase." This proves conclusively that SBA borrowers are excellent repayers. It also shows that the bank industry couldn't care less.

SBA conducts a sustained campaign to get the banks moving. With the recent decline in interest rates increasing the competition for loan business among banks, a recent SBA study showed that over half the nation's banks have participated in small business loans. However, that leaves nearly 7,000 banks, each of which must have many potential small business customers, which have yet to cooperate with the SBA even once.

Requiring you to be turned down by a bank before SBA enters the picture is a joke. Any bank will quickly come up with reasons why they cannot make your loan if they smell SBA assistance in the background. Why shouldn't they? If SBA *guarantees* the loan, the bank's exposure is substantially lowered, even though it costs the bank ½ of 1% to have SBA assume its risk.

Before counting too heavily on SBA assistance, check its current ability to loan. Its funds are limited to a revolving pool which is replenished only by loan repayments or supplemental appropriations by Congress. Several times it has had to declare a moratorium. On other occasions it has tightened standards to limit the number and amount of loans. This is the first thing to determine if you are considering an SBA loan. Here is another.

Loan Priorities

With over 14 million small businesses in the country the Small Business Administration cannot, of course, meet the needs of all the firms that seek funds. In order to use its resources more effectively, SBA makes loans on a priority basis. These loans, in order of priority, are:

1. Loans to businesses in defense-oriented industries.
2. Loans to businesses that plan to increase employment substantially or to businesses in designated depressed areas.
3. Loans to businesses which help reduce our balance of payments deficit through export sales.
4. Loans to businesses which help reduce air and water pollution.
5. Loans determined to be in the public interest on the basis of local economic needs.

Small firms in any of these categories are helping to meet national goals and local needs. These are factors SBA considers when reviewing loan requests.

Despite its problems, SBA has been a tremendous help to small business. As lending institutions go, it is huge. On assets alone it would be the 19th largest bank in the U.S., according to *Fortune*'s ratings. Since nearly all its assets are loanable, its ability to loan would rate even higher.

Small Business Investment Companies

SBICs are not well known or understood. They do not operate everywhere. Most of them are involved in an extremely small number of loans, and only about a thousand have been chartered up to now. Recent indications are that they are *not* doing well.

An offspring of SBA, SBICs are private investment companies which supply small firms with equity capital and long-term financing. They are private and not connected with SBA directly. Their formation is part of the law which established and governs SBA, and part of their capital has been loaned to *them* by SBA. SBICs are intended to encourage private investment in small business.

SBIC owners must put up a minimum of $350,000 initial capital—and the SBA will match that by loan, to give the company minimum assets of $700,000. As "security" for the SBA loan the SBICs give subordinated debentures. (Wouldn't you like the government to buy a few subordinated debentures in your business?)

In short, SBIC regulations are aimed at getting together as much capital as possible so these funds can be loaned to small business.

Another way SBIC differs—which may be vital to you —is that they usually want an option to buy stock in your business. They also purchase debentures and make loans. The money they provide must be for a term of at least five years and can go as long as twenty. SBICs are under some regulation, such as the percentage of assets they may loan to a single borrower. By and large, they operate in the most liberal financing climate of any money-lender serving small business.

In view of this it is reasonable to expect SBIC to be the answer to small business prayers. So far it hasn't worked out that way. SBIC operators have often been as cautious as banks. They have frequently been just plain greedy. Instead of purchasing shares, for example, some SBICs have reportedly offered "loans" instead. Interest rates have been as high as 15% as authorized by law. In addition, the SBIC frequently demands stock so it will have a voice in operating the company.

SBIC could help small business to normal growth and profits. Hopefully when it becomes a few years older it will outgrow the problems and become a positive force. Meanwhile, if there is an SBIC in your area check it out. It may already be mature.

MESBICs

Minority Enterprise Small Business Investment Companies, another program administered by the Small Business Administration, annually provide more than $35 million in financing to concerns owned by blacks, Hispanics, women, and Vietnam veterans. From the program's inception in 1968 through the first quarter of 1982, more than 230 MESBICs were funded. While 72 failed, the remaining companies were flourishing, with more than $130 million of capitalization and an additional $140 million in credit lines available from the SBA. The MESBIC program permits minority entrepreneurs who successfully pass the stringent credit checks to obtain up to $150,000 of MESBIC financing and up to $300,000 more in SBA loans. Among the projects handled by the program are leveraged buyouts in Eastern industrial centers, second-stage financing for black-owned manufacturing and service businesses in the Midwest, and providing operating capital for Mexican-American-owned oil-related businesses in the Southwest.

Friends and Relatives

A well-off friend, or relative, who can afford a risk is the last resort. Human nature being what it is, mixing business and family or business and friends is dangerous. It invites personal conflicts. The business and the personal relationship can both be ruined when personalities get in-volved. But—it is often better to risk this than slowing the company's growth momentum or closing the business.

Leasing Your Own Equipment or Real Estate

Another way of obtaining funds to finance your busi-ness is to sell some of your equipment and lease it back. This should be carefully considered before doing it. Check with your lawyer and accountant.

There are many leasing companies throughout the country. Leasing is a big business, and it has become big-ger in recent years. (You should also consider *leasing* rather than *buying* new capital equipment.)

Some of the advantages of leasing your own equipment are as follows:

1. Provides instant cash.
2. The rental (usually monthly payments) is a deductible expense to your business.
3. Your financial statement is improved.
4. You have obtained more *long*-term capital.

All you do is call a leasing company, show him the equipment you are using, and convince him that you can make the payments. He will pay you nearly any reasonable price that you suggest.

What are the disadvantages of leasing your own or new equipment?

1. It is quite an expensive way of borrowing money. Most leasing companies borrow large sums from banks, paying prime interest rates, and have to charge you for this, plus their overhead risks, and profit. Compare this cost with regular borrowing and be sure you know what you are getting in for.

2. You lose the amortization of your capital equipment, taxwise. Compare this with the cost of leasing.

3. At the end of lease (three to five years or more), taking title back on the equipment is tricky, taxwise. After you have made all the payments, the leasing company may let you reown the equipment for $1.00. This may be challenged by the IRS. Some leasing companies have tricky ways of helping you here, such as giving you a separate agreement or perhaps a verbal understanding.

4. Your equipment will be tagged, or labeled, that it is owned by the leasing company.

5. Your equipment now is not available to use as collateral with another lender. Before looking into leasing, be sure this equipment is not already included as collateral (chattel mortgage) with your bank. Ask your banker for *"advice"* on this; you will probably have to get his permission anyway.

One further thought that the entrepreneur should ponder along the way. If small businesses were aided by government because we had a political pressure group, banks would be right in there resisting. But small business is not organized at all. Government help is being given small business because it is essential to the economy, locally and nationally. It is also a keystone of our democracy since it is the starting point of free enterprise. When anyone opposes efforts to aid this vital segment of our national life —banker or otherwise—he is not merely opposing a government policy but damaging the fabric of American life. *These* are the reasons government has every right to insist that banks get on with the job of helping small business.

This is not to suggest unsound loans be required of banks or any lender. The businessman should have to prove his case before getting a loan. He ought to be able to get one, however, if he can show that the risk is prudently calculated and that he has a good statistical chance of success. At least a limited percentage of such "growth loans" should be available.

Bankers have rationalized their position by talk about "protecting their depositors' funds" and "keeping the bank from failing." Their arguments do carry more weight in recent years, since the number of banks failures has soared from 6 in 1977 to 80 in 1984, and the number of banks in trouble has increased from 368 to 848 in the same period of time. At the same time, however, the more than 14,000 banks that aren't in trouble earned $15 billion in 1984, and many well-run institutions are getting stronger and stronger.

If your banker grows skittish about a loan, never hesitate to approach other money lenders. Financing is where you find it. And it might just be that you don't need your banker as badly as you thought.

PART TWO

SELECTING PROFESSIONAL SERVICES

CHAPTER VI

Lawyers:
The Pursed-Mouth
Fraternity

THE first step in starting a small business is to see a lawyer. The SBA reports a vast majority of small businesses are unincorporated. Why? Don't they have lawyers? Or are lawyers failing to convince small businessmen of the advantages of incorporating?

Your lawyer should be clerk or secretary of your corporation. He can keep the minutes, file the required reports, and generally handle the detail you hire him for—without bothering you. Frequently he is made a director also. Since he will be intimately associated with you, possibly for a long time, choosing the right lawyer is important. There are many good lawyers, but few are versed in small business.

Most lawyers provide more negative help than positive. Their standard reasoning begins, "According to the statutes . . ." In general they try to keep you out of trouble and guide you away from pitfalls. They are usually not entrepreneurs. In fact, they are frequently poor businessmen.

Frequently lawyers' office routines are poorly organized. They fail to send out bills on time, write poor letters, their bills are not detailed, and their desks are piled high with pending material. If it were not for their legal secretaries they would be out of business!

Lawyers are professional men, highly educated at great time and expense. They seem to share a slight disdain for the ordinary small businessman. And if you are really successful, they cannot quite understand it.

Successful lawyers have larger clients who require most of their time and pay most of their income. At best, your little business is going to get a very small percentage of his effort.

Seldom will he suggest what you should do but rather what you should not do. It is up to you to stimulate him with suggestions. Try them on him for his comments. Your suggestions may be far out, but don't worry about it. Sometimes a really far-out idea can be a very profitable one.

When your lawyer gives you advice you need not necessarily follow it. Ask him why. Make him explain his reasons—all the pros and cons. After you thoroughly understand his reasoning you still may want to proceed against his advice but knowing full well the possible consequences.

Lawyers are constantly exposed to unreasonable, recalcitrant, and dishonest individuals, involved bankruptcies and other manifestations of man's less noble side. It makes them pessimists. These human traits keep them in business. And when one of us small businessmen goes broke, the lawyer usually makes out quite well in the bankruptcy proceedings.

Apparently being negative pays. Lawyers are the most

negative of the necessary, unproductive professional vendors you need in your business.

Choosing a Lawyer

If you do not have confidence in your lawyer, or do not
have one, meet with two or three. This helps you to get the
one who best fits your need.

Personalities are of some importance. It may help you
feel more confident if you and your lawyer get along in a
friendly fashion. But hire him for business, not friendship.

By all means, do not mix business and pleasure where
your lawyer is concerned. You will both be better served if
you remain merely business associates.

Did you ever try getting a quotation from a lawyer as
you would from any other supplier? Or even a rough esti-
mate? You could pick up the phone and call ten lawyers to
ask for a quote on incorporating a small business. It is
doubtful one would give you an answer. Instead, you will
be asked to "come to my office to talk about it." You want
to know what it is going to cost, so you go.

A conference takes place. Most of the talk is general,
some of it merely getting acquainted. He takes copious
notes and asks direct, leading questions. You end up bar-
ing your soul under his trained probing. Before you know
it you owe him nine hundred bucks for "conference time"
and all you wanted to know was the cost of incorporating.
He has you trapped. You have told him all your problems
and secrets and run up $100 on his meter. You've got
yourself a lawyer, whether you wanted him or not.

Ironically, your investigatory visit is the most costly for
the attorney. He actually puts in the time with you then
and you know he does because you are there. *Doing* your

work might not take that long. The practice of law is often a business in which "boiler plate" forms can be cranked out on a mimeograph. Your lawyer has done it a hundred times or more.

After he "converts" you to a client, you may wait days and weeks while nothing happens. Finally you call and ask why. He says he has been busy on it and is now going to "dispense with your matter" in the next few days. Translated, that means he was busy on other things but will now do something for you since you prodded him.

He calls in his secretary and says, "Will you draw up a corporation for that fellow Smythe?"

"What are the details?" she inquires.

"Well," he says, "remember the one we did for Joe Blow and Company?"

"Yes, it's in the file."

"Fine, make it just like that one."

The end. As soon as the typist copies off the details, changing only the name and a few facts, then mails it to the State House, with the fee, you will be incorporated.

If you are wondering whether it took years of law school for that, the answer is yes. It *must* be the extra education that does it, because you and I can't get away with it and we have everything he's got except the law school training.

The brightest guys do not always make the best practicing attorneys. There is a law school saying that ...

A students make professors
B students make judges
C students make money

This bears out a few observations about lawyers in general, especially the C students, who constitute the bulk of practicing attorneys.

They, the C students, probably more than any other professional group, depend heavily on their alma mater, at least insofar as their former classmates are concerned. For instance, you may go to your attorney with a legal matter out of state. He reaches for a very special book listing all lawyers in the U.S. The first thing he looks for in the town where you need representation is a classmate. Other requirements are less important. The school he attended makes this lawyer just the guy to handle your case.

This publication—*The Martindale-Hubbell Law Directory*—has a remarkable way of classifying lawyers for other lawyers that tells a lot about the legal profession. It is like a D & B report, complete with credit rating and net worth. It purports to advise whether so-and-so is a good lawyer. Which implies that some, or maybe many, members of the bar are not good.

The greater the net worth of a lawyer, the better he is implied to be. He might have inherited it. His law school is also of first importance. While the Harvard Law grad may get the better rating and be the choice of your attorney (because that's *his* alma mater), there is probably a better-qualified man for your case in Timbuktu who only graduated from East Overshoe Law School.

"Fee Building": How Much to Pay a Lawyer

Perhaps the most popular course in law school today is reputedly one the students call "fee building." It teaches an aspiring attorney how to wring the most income out of each case. Caveat emptor ("buyer beware"), the ancient rallying cry for the battle between buyer and seller, applies equally to lawyers and other members of the professions.

It is up to you to beware your lawyer because you are the buyer. Ask for estimates of the cost of everything

he does. If he doesn't like it, remind him you have to run
your company on a tight budget or else there wouldn't *be*
any money to pay him. Question any bills you do not
thoroughly understand and request a detailed breakdown.

Do this in a friendly way. The charges may be reasonable when explained. He has to make a living too. Also,
you may dampen his enthusiasm for handling your matters. Unfortunately, most business lawyers who become
disenchanted will not suggest you get another attorney.
They do not want to lose the income. Instead, the enthusiasm and quality of their work just goes to pot.

You may want to give your lawyer stock in lieu of a fee
for incorporating your small business. This opportunity
will be quickly accepted by some attorneys who realize
they cannot become wealthy on the income from legal
practice. They may want, also, a chance to make capital
gains.

If your lawyer does not buy this suggestion, better re-
examine your business just to be sure. He may be trying to
tell you he sees flaws or problems. Maybe not. He may not
yet be in a position of affording capital gains, especially if
he is a young lawyer and has a big family, or has business
interests of his own for which he needs operating cash.
"Partner policy" may rule it out in some law firms. But try
it. The object of offering stock—in addition to saving cash
when you need it most—is to obtain his special interest.
Your chances of putting this deal across may be better
with your second or third business, after your lawyer has
seen you make a success of your first one.

If your lawyer will agree to handle all your work for a
yearly retainer, that may seem like a good deal. Sometimes it is. But you get what you pay for in the long run. If
you require little legal assistance during the year, it is a

bad deal for you. If you need a lot it is bad for the lawyer. Deals in which either side is dissatisfied usually go sour.

Since a retainer is a gamble on both sides, it must be thoroughly discussed and understood. Finally, it must be further agreed that the fee can be adjusted the following year to compensate whichever party got the worst of the deal. There are tax angles here. You may want the expense and he may want the income in one year. Or vice versa.

It is simpler and cheaper not to bother with a retainer in most cases. Let the lawyer bill you for his time and that's that. When you use him, you pay. This arrangement only becomes a disadvantage when you avoid using your lawyer in order to save a few bucks. The availability of legal counsel for all necessary matters is the prime advantage of a retainer. When you retain your lawyer you will use him more frequently.

Contingency fees are another question. When your lawyer takes up to one-third of the settlement for his fee, it hurts. Especially if it is a collection matter where you are already the loser. On the other hand, would your lawyer pursue the case as hard, and refuse to make settlement, if he were on an hourly rate? Maybe he would work just as hard either way.

From the lawyer's viewpoint, a contingency fee is the only way he can be an entrepreneur within his profession. He invests in your case when he takes it on contingency. He has got to be sure he wins and gets top dollar in order to profit on his investment.

If you pay your lawyer on an hourly basis, you have to pay him, win or lose. Despite his best efforts, you could lose.

Until you work on a long hard case with them you do

not realize how diligently good lawyers perform for their clients. I went through one of the longest and largest lawsuits in my state a few years ago and I came out of it a staunch admirer of the attorneys in the case. Not just my own (who had the satisfaction of winning) but the other side also. Both did an excellent job.

One of small business' problems with lawyers is that it often takes a really important case to challenge them to their best. Small business provides few of those. Most of its legal needs are run-of-the-mill.

Lawyers are all in close touch with one another. In court they put on a good front of fighting for you, but out of court they have friendly meetings about your case. Over cocktails at the bar (not the legal one) they often decide your future. You may wonder whose side your lawyer is on!

They nearly always exclude you from the final negotiations of a settlement. You wait in another room—or by a phone in another city—while they, in their mysterious ways, "work things out."

Lawyers give the impression that they and they alone are set apart from the rest of the business world. Don't believe it! They step into their trousers one leg at a time just as you do, the only difference being that they do it slower, with a bit more deliberation.

Do the Laws Favor Lawyers?

In some states anyone can attach anyone's bank account at any time, for any reason. Everyone agrees such extreme practices are unfair and against our concepts of being innocent until proven guilty. Every state also has outmoded laws affecting small business that need to be eliminated or updated. Yet it takes action by the state legislature to change them and very little attention is paid by the lawmakers. Why? A large percentage of legislators are lawyers. They profit from such laws. Attorneys themselves obviously are not going to lobby to change unfair laws, such as the attachment statutes, when these very laws bring clients into their offices.

Here is an example of how laws favor the lawyers. At a critical period of one of my small businesses, it was attached for $32,000, tying up, for six months, its real estate, equipment, and bank accounts. The attachment froze all our current working capital. I finally did get a bond to free the bank account but at a high price.

Lawyers for both sides conferred for six months and got nowhere. The plaintiff, a former sales representative of mine, claimed he was owed $1,500. We claimed it was $300.

We had recently moved to a new plant which happened to be in another state. Apparently, feeling this move across the state line had somehow harmed his position, the sales representative called his attorney. That "gentleman" referred the case (probably using the *Martindale-Hubbell Directory*) to a lawyer in the small town to which we had moved.

The local attorney sat on it for over a month. At that time my company, having settled in its new quarters, announced an open house to get acquainted with our new neighbors, employees, and their wives. Proud of the new small industry in their town, all the big shots, including the mayor, showed up for the official opening of the plant. At precisely the moment set for cutting the ribbon, the sheriff also attended—uninvited. He plastered sheriff's notices on the front door, on all the larger machinery and equipment, helped himself to the free coffee and doughnuts, and left.

I finally got tired of waiting for the lawyers. After six months, and all the embarrassment, I put through a person-to-person call to the other guy . . . and, *over the phone*, settled the claim for $500. Then we each called our own attorneys and advised them that we had settled it and, therefore, would the lawyers follow through on the routine paperwork ASAP.

This violated the standard advice, handed out mainly by lawyers, never to go over or around your attorney. But if I had done that in the first place I would have saved a big legal bill and the embarrassing open-house fiasco. I never did find out whether the local attorney was ever paid by his out-of-state client.

Some laws, like the attachment statute, are unfair. If mine had been a retail business serving the local public, the sheriff's notices could have put us out of business. It is the law that is wrong. But it is the lawyers' fault that it is still on the books. And it is lawyers who resort to using it and have been for two hundred years.

Most politicians are lawyers. Thus, lawyers are the ones who make the laws. This is against the entire principle of protective government and the regulative bodies it sets up. The Interstate Commerce Commission regulates the transportation industry, bank examiners regulate the banks, and so on. For lawyers it is just the opposite. Members of their own profession regulate the laws from which they make their living. Incidentally, did you ever hear of one lawyer suing another one?

If your company is going through a rough period financially, and you fall behind in paying some of your bills, the ever-active rumor mill may panic one of your less sophisticated creditors. He may put your account in the hands of the lawyers. Once *they* get it you are in for trouble.

In the settlement of an estate, even a small one, lawyers usually take their time (money). They frequently do not file the final account until they have to (present law, nine months). Many large estates take longer and extensions are easily obtained from the courts. It appears that the longer they take the higher a fee can be justified.

Put Your Lawyer to Work

A man had an occurrence recently that illustrates how closely you may have to watch your lawyer to get the proper work out of him. He had a fire at his place of business which was then under construction. There was insufficient insurance, and rather than wait to see how things worked out the contractor got panicky and attached everything the man had: real estate, car, business, everything. This proved unnecessary as the man had ample finances, and the matter was settled despite the shortage of insurance.

Several years later the man decided to sell some acreage he had owned for many years. A buyer was found, the price agreed on after the usual dickering, and papers were ready to pass. Suddenly the buyer's attorney discovered that the land was still under attachment. The man found out that the attachment put on everything by the frightened contractor several years earlier had never been lifted.

His attorney said, "Oh, I guess we forgot to release the attachment when we settled that case."

Lawyers make their living from detail. Often this demonstrates how surprisingly poor they are at handling detail. To overcome this, small business practitioners must have a definite plan for putting a lawyer to work and then checking his output.

The first step in getting good work out of your attorney is to choose one who is capable and honest.

The next is to arrange to pay him in a manner that gives him an incentive and secures his wholehearted interest in your business(es).

Another important rule is to work closely with your lawyer. If you call him after trouble is brewing, obviously it will take more time, and cost more, than if he can head off the trouble before it starts.

Do not try to be a lawyer yourself. Be an ignorant small business pro and do what comes naturally, because it is the intent that counts under our laws.

But do not let your attorney run the show either. Override him when it makes sense. *You* make the decisions. His job is to outline the alternatives so you can do so intelligently.

CHAPTER VII

The Historians
of Business

ACCOUNTANTS are necessary—but usually unproductive as far as any original thinking is concerned. The reason they are necessary was expressed by a famous philosopher who said, "Life can only be understood backwards, but must be lived forwards." Like lawyers, accountants will rarely call, or come dashing into your office, with a new or creative idea. They are not built that way. If they were, they would not be accountants.

What does an accountant really do for your business? He gathers past information, collates, and puts it in commonly accepted form. Since money is the way a business keeps score, these historical records are important. Accountants are the historians of business.

Like all historians, they are primarily concerned with the past. The time period in which your accountant is concentrating is one which you cannot do much about. It is too late. You either did or did not make your profit last year. That is over now—and has become the exclusive property of the accountants and the IRS.

It is important to keep records. In fact, it is a legal requirement. Because they are essential to pay taxes, among other uses, your records must be accurate. Since he is the one responsible for their accuracy, your accountant spends much of his time "correcting papers." But bear in mind, accountants are largely negative thinkers and, like lawyers, have multiple reasons why you cannot do this or that.

Proportional Pay

Your accountant will tell you that employees should be paid in proportion to their contribution. The first person to whom you should apply that rule is your accountant.

Because he is a professional, small businessmen stand in awe of the accountant—especially if he is a CPA who functions as an auditor on a vendor basis. As usual, this awe is awfully expensive.

History has its value. We do—or can—learn from the past. Yet you, and presumably your employees, are living in the present, trying to make a profit today. To do so you must have records which are accessible and, in turn, you need to know how to use them. That is where accountants come in.

But if they only *keep* records and do not make them easy for you to use, you are not getting what you are paying for. To many accountants, keeping the records is an end in itself. They are not accountants at all, but bookkeepers.

It is important to distinguish between the two. A bookkeeper is a technician but not a professional. He, or usually she, has some training. Her job is simply to keep records. Because this is an unproductive job, a necessary but unprofitable expenditure, the bookkeeper's pay need be only what it takes to get the job done and out of the way.

An accountant is a professional with special education, usually a college or business school degree in the subject. If he intends to set up a practice, or work in an accounting firm, the graduate accountant will usually take a state test to become a Certified Public Accountant. This is his license to practice, except that it is not necessary in all cases as, for example, a doctor's license is. No doctor can spend one minute practicing without a license. CPA licensing is not that strict but intended primarily for those who have their own practice. Accountants who work as employees in industry do not need CPA licensing, though some get it for the prestige and, usually, a higher salary.

Many bookkeepers work their way up to company controller or treasurer by improving their skills and knowledge with or without a CPA. If a bookkeeper cannot handle your accounting workload, do you need a true, college-trained accountant? Or can a person who learned accounting without formal training suffice? As a rule there is a difference in cost, the college-trained accountant demanding more money, just as a regular accountant is worth more than a bookkeeper.

You must weigh this difference carefully if you want to get all you are paying for. A sheepskin is no guarantee of superiority over skill picked up the hard way. Often the opposite is true: the nongraduate realizes he is at a disadvantage and will work harder to make up for it.

If your business is of a size that needs outside accounting help, in addition to or in place of your accounting department, then you may want to engage a CPA. Even a very small business needs him once a year for the IRS.

There are no rules to tell when to switch from a bookkeeper to a hired accountant, or whether to augment your bookkeeping by buying outside public accounting services instead. There are countless variations in the combinations of bookkeeper, accountant, public accountant, and auditor.

Accountants have one thing going for them, namely, the income tax laws. If it were not for tax problems and preparation, their importance would be somewhat less. Everyone, and especially small businessmen, lives in fear of making a mistake in their tax returns. Around filing time, the CPA is king. Obviously, that is the wrong time to make overtures about hiring one.

Tax laws make work for accountants. This, in turn, forces us to hire and put a higher value on our accountants. Uncle Sam not only takes it from us in taxes but also for the personnel and overhead to figure how much we have to pay.

How do you bring your outside accountant truly into your team? One way is to pay him only partly in salary. Give him the rest of his incentive in stock. That way it becomes his company too, and he cannot help but care how the company is doing; he will be more likely to contribute some forward thinking.

The negative thinking and dispassionate objectivity which made him become an accountant will not disappear —you don't want them to. To a degree they are valuable. Offering your accountant some stock will cause him to draw more closely into the business and care about the things you do.

If your accountant refuses to accept such an arrangement, his insecurity is showing. Or yours! For he, of all people, should know that salaries cannot make wealth, whereas capital gains can.

Turn Negative into Positive

Usually members of the professions make lousy businessmen. They understand the professional part all right, but the business emphasis escapes them. They are specialists rather than the generalists pro businessmen must be.

But that's all right. In fact, it works out well for both sides. Accountants are human computers. Since computers are now common in some CPA offices, the progressive ones are beginning to provide more than just history. Tax advice and financial planning are becoming more urgent, and a CPA who spends time with you on such matters can be invaluable.

If you had the time to read and understand all the financial reports published each week, you would not need the average accountant. Except for once a year to do your annual statement and your tax return—the most important thing your accountant can offer.

> *When you look for an accountant look for a tax man,*
> *for if you are successful in making a profit, up to 34%*
> *of it may go to Uncle.*

Don't be afraid to overrule your accountant's suggestion even where accounting judgment is concerned. You still have to make the final decisions. That is the cost of leadership. The best accountants will go by the book, and the past, and by what others are doing—and will seldom come up with anything new for you to consider. This forces you to make the decisions when the chips are down. What you need from your accountant are some well-thought-out alternatives.

Do not forget to let him help you interpret your financial statements. If you do not understand your own statements, it should be his fault, not yours. Ask him to help; perhaps he can help you avoid making last year's mistakes again.

It may be of interest to ask the question, "Why are certain people and corporations investigated by the IRS, while the vast majority are not?" Since all our tax returns are on computers now, what can the computer do? Can a computer tell when an expense account is unreasonable? Can a computer tell whether or not your inventory is under- or overpriced?

The one thing a computer *can* do is observe any substantial change. If your figures remain relatively the same each year, there is no problem. But, if there is a considerable change in any portion of your tax return, a red light flashes somewhere in the inner sanctum. If you suddenly show a large (increased) profit one year, or an unusually large loss, watch out! There is much to be said for a certified audit each year, and especially so if you anticipate any substantial changes. A CPA signing the return along with your signature, may help.

CHAPTER VIII

Professional Purveyors and Purchasing Pitfalls

BUSINESS consists of buying and selling. Business generates income by selling . . . but it can lose money buying.

Purchasing Techniques

The first rule for all purchasing—pencils or bank loans—is to have multiple sources. Establish two or more sources for every item of supply or service if you possibly can. With multiple sources, chances are increased for getting delivery on time and at the right price. It saves time in case your normal supplier, for any reason, lets you down and you must find an alternate. More important, you will get superior service from alternate sources who have been calling on you regularly, waiting for their chance to get your business.

Invite alternate sources to call on you even if you do not intend to use them immediately. If their prices, quality, service, attitude, and other factors are equivalent to your present supply, level with them by saying you have a vendor but want them to keep in touch since you may split your business or make a change. Any supplier worth your consideration will go out of his way trying to get your business under those circumstances.

You may find one who wants your order badly enough to make concessions on price, delivery, etcetera. You may discover that your present supplier is not giving you the best deal. Alternate sources keep present suppliers on their toes at no cost to you other than an occasional chat with salesmen.

One attitude that stamps a small businessman as an amateur is unfriendliness to the salesmen calling on him. The salesmen who solicit your business can be a major source of information about prices, new products, competitive developments, and many other factors you need to know. No matter how closely you study your market and industry, you cannot get inside your competitors' plants and offices the way these salesmen can. Listen to them and learn what is really going on.

It is possible to spend too much time with salesmen, of course. Good ones understand when you are unable to see them. Ask them to make an appointment; they usually do anyway because they do not want to waste their own time either. We should see other company salesmen because we want other companies to see ours.

For small businessmen it is good policy to make an effort selling *your* company to salesmen who call on you. If they hear progress, new customers, growth, and confidence every time they are in your place of business, they will sell their credit people on working with you. To small business, for which tight money is a way of life, this can be worth thousands of dollars in credit. Salesmen who call on you can be one of your best and least expensive forms of public relations.

In manufacturing the question frequently arises whether

to buy or make. Volumes of highly technical advice have been written on the topic, but the average small manufacturer has not time to study the subject in its entirety. Besides, most of the published material is written by professionals for big business.

Small businessmen are forced to rely on common sense and their own intuition when this question comes up. For example, if you are a manufacturer of radio equipment, it would be absurd to manufacture your own tubes, transistors, and similar parts. But, if your business is a car wash, is it equally absurd to make your own soap? *It might not be.* If you hit upon a really good soap formula for this specialized purpose, perhaps you should consider making it or having it made for you. Not for yourself alone, however, but to start a *new* business which sells your new soap nationally to other car washes.

Many successful small businesses got started this way, from an offshoot or side product of the original business.

Most small businessmen are sufficiently credit-conscious to run checks on their customers. It is also important to run credit checks on suppliers and potential vendors! If a supplier of an important item is not sound financially, he may be unable to deliver at a crucial time.

Most small businesses cannot afford and do not need to subscribe to Dun & Bradstreet or other credit reporting services. Your banker does, and as part of his service will get reports for you. Usually banks charge their cost for doing this, but not always. Set up an arrangement to use your bank D & B service with the vice-president, so he will know you follow good purchasing and credit policies. But arrange to handle it through a clerk so you do not have to be involved with the officer every time you need this service.

It is almost always more profitable to buy top quality,

whether it is bolts or legal advice. The worst that can happen is that you will have to work a little harder to afford it.

Don't worry about who is taking advantage of you; spend more of your time finding out whom you can take advantage of!

This is not to say you should not watch your suppliers, but proportion the amount of time you spend at it. Your business makes its profits by selling, not buying. In 1982, according to Dun & Bradstreet, 39.0% of the 24,900 business failures were attributed to inadequate sales, whereas only 11.1% were due to "excessive expenditures."

The Credit Factor in Purchasing

You need to know how to handle suppliers in the matter of credit, which is, in fact, borrowing from them.

If you seek long-term credit—dating, as it is sometimes called—be sure there is no cost attached. Or if there is, that it is reasonable. The best dating is when extended terms are allowed as an incentive to close the sale at no extra cost. Approach it this way with your supplier. Let him know the terms you must have if he wants the deal. If he says no, try your alternative sources. If none of them accept your terms, you may have to back down. As a rule you will not have to back all the way down to their regular terms. What is more, you put them on their toes by serving notice that you expect the best service and terms. Good suppliers will meet this challenge.

Using trade credit stretches your working capital. This is not to say extended terms are always a good thing. If suppliers allow a discount for payment with order, by all means take the discount if you can. Also any discount for prompt payment. A lost 2% discount can be costly over a year. The latest trend now being used nationally by manufacturers, as well as retailers, is the *opposite* of the prompt payment discount. They now charge you 1½% per month if you *do not* pay promptly. This is 18% per year. If your business is not doing this, you probably should be.

In trade credit, as in all borrowing, there comes a day of reckoning. The biggest credit error small businessmen make is buying things on credit which they really cannot afford.

The payment *will* fall due and one failure to pay may seriously hurt your company.

When a business is very young or in a tight position, you may have to take a chance. It is sounder to take the risk to obtain an essential shipment than to suffer more harm by doing without it. If the payment date comes around and things have not sufficiently improved, there is one more out: refinancing. Often the creditor will be willing to rewrite the deal if he sees you have made progress as well as an honest effort to pay him. Do not avoid him, however. Call him *before* he calls you. Tell him your problem—chances are he will try to help.

Management failure, including not knowing what debt the company can safely incur, is the largest single cause of all business failures, according to Dun & Bradstreet.

Fortunately there are some natural checks that prevent you from getting too deeply in debt. Perhaps suppliers will not extend credit and banks may not let you borrow. But if they do, watch your step.

The greatest change in our way of doing business has been the increased availability and importance of credit. Fairchild Publications quips, "Debt has joined the ranks of those other inevitables, death and taxes." The small businessman who does not utilize trade credit to the maximum safe level for his situation may place himself at a competitive disadvantage. Like financing, credit is where you find it. But you have to keep looking. Suppliers hardly ever broach the subject themselves, not while you are small, that is.

CHAPTER IX

Actual
or Actuarial

INSURANCE is a negative thing. You are betting against yourself. But you have to. You need it personally and you need it in your business.

Insurance companies have done very well over the years. They have many strong advantages that they use successfully to keep growing and accumulating tremendous wealth. Much of this has been gained at the expense of small businesses and individuals.

Liability and Casualty Insurance

Among the advantages an insurance company has over small businessmen are these:

1. The "fine print." Insurance companies, over the years, have developed legal departments which are very capable—capable of protecting the insurance company. They have years of experience in the courts, usually as the *defendant*. They can afford litigation better and longer than you can. They have developed paragraphs of fine print which are so tricky that frequently their own "salesman" (agent) cannot fully explain their entire significance.

If you have a loss, an expert from the home office is

called in and very simply interprets the "fine print."
Chances are you will not agree with this explanation. But
your "friendly agent" sits back, shakes his head, and says,
"You know how it is," trying to remain friendly. Of
course, when your agent sold you the policy neither he nor
you had the time or the ability to go into it thoroughly.

You do not get to look at the "fine print" (unless you
specifically ask for it) until *after* you have made your
purchase. You are really buying a "pig in a poke" because
your policy arrives with your bill! You have already
bought it and been invoiced *before* you get to see the final
product.

2. *The no-sell "salesman."* Actually, did your agent *sell*
you the insurance in the first place? Chances are he did
not. Why? Because most insurance men are not salesmen.
They are order takers with the title of agent or broker.

Most businesses really have to sell their products. Insurance men do not, because everyone has to have some.
Your "friendly agent" is not usually a good salesman anyway. Since he is offering a negative product, chances are
he is a negative-type guy—not the real extrovert needed to
be a salesman in other industries. That is probably why he
is selling insurance instead of another item. Could he sell
your product, for example?

Chances are he did not sell you enough insurance in the
beginning. He "gets" your insurance and delivers, or mails,
you the policies, then seldom checks back often enough
to take the responsibility you placed in him. Your business
changes very rapidly. You are busy making it change. Insurance is seldom given enough thought aside from making the premium payments. You do not give your insurance more than a casual glance once or twice a year. It
cannot build your business.

Where is that "friendly agent" in whom you placed your confidence? Why isn't he selling you constantly—updating, changing, suggesting, and helping you cover all your potential areas of loss? Doesn't he want to sell you more insurance?

One day you have a loss. He is Johnny-on-the-spot then—but to protect the insurance company interests. Despite the ads which assure that he will look out for you, he is really there to get an immediate look at the loss to be sure his company does not pay one penny more than they have to. And to collect any possible evidence to show it was really your fault and not covered by the policy. You take the policy home and try to read it. You cannot understand much of it.

Next day he tries to explain. He uses phrases such as: "I didn't know that you opened up a new department," "You didn't tell me about this," "If I had known that this was what you wanted," or "You could have had that coverage if you had asked for it."

This puts the burden of adequate liability and casualty insurance on you. The only way you can shift the burden is to find that rarity, an insurance agent who is either a sales personality or a sufficiently good detail man to keep your coverage abreast of your growth and changes. To enable him to do so, recognize that he is not a salesman and will not keep after you the way other salesmen do. Make it clear to him, at the beginning, exactly what you expect of him. Invite him to visit your business regularly, talk with your employees, and keep in very close touch with what is going on.

Being overinsured is also wasteful, since all insurance is a necessary waste and totally unproductive. The burden is on you, again, to avoid being insurance-poor.

3. *The double agent.* One of the prominent recent ad campaigns has been in behalf of the independent insurance agent. This is the broker, the one who represents several companies, as opposed to the company agent who is employed by a single company or insurance group and sells its policies only.

The ads have emphasized the benefits of an agent who is not beholden to a single company but can concentrate on representing you. He can place your policies with whichever company offers the best deal for your specific needs. In theory this makes sense. Invite an independent agent to detail the benefits for you if you are now buying from a company man.

Chances are, however, that you are already insured through an independent, since they are in the majority. They are also the ones most interested in small business, being small businessmen themselves—and finding it difficult to compete with company men.

There are disadvantages. A recent case in which a fire loss occurred to a newly acquired piece of property will serve as an example. The owner had covered the building with a binder by telephone as soon as he signed the papers.

(Get a binder on anything which needs coverage as soon as you purchase it. All it takes is a telephone call. True, you have no legal record of having ordered the coverage. You are completely at the mercy of your agent. But the system is such a convenience to them that instances of abuse are rare. If you are dubious, you can always have one or two people witness the call.)

Several weeks elapsed. The agent had not gotten the policy to the small businessman. The building caught fire. The agent attended the fire and watched the fire department put out the blaze, which extensively damaged the structure. The next day he delivered the policies. After the fire!

Had the policies been made out before the fire? Or were they hastily drawn up afterwards? In ordering the binder the owner had left details of the coverage to the agent. What coverage had he chosen? What fire insurance company did he choose (he represented several)? Why did he decide on a certain one? Did he choose a company with whom he had many losses? Or few losses? Did he decide on a company that was about to drop him anyway? Or he to drop them? Did he have any selfish motivations? Did he decide on a company which usually pays its claims promptly without any prolonged argument? Or otherwise?

There was no "fine print" in the binder, a simple telephone call. But there was considerable "fine print" in the policies delivered the day after the fire.

Were the agent's best interests served by fighting for his customer? Taking a middle-of-the-road position? Or perhaps looking out for the company?

This was an unusual situation, but it points out the consideration the independent agent faces when he places your business among the several companies he represents. Your problem is to be certain his primary concern is for *you*, not himself or the companies. You have almost no information on which to form an opinion. You are at his mercy.

In your business career, how many fire or other losses have you had? Probably few, if any, so your "friendly agent" remains your friend. Wait until you have a loss and an adjustor enters the picture. Then observe with whom your agent is "friendly."

The Adjustor. For whom does this so-called independent adjustor work? Where does he obtain his salary (or perhaps commission)? Is he really independent? The successful adjustor is not one who gives out liberal claims; he is the man who fights hard for the insurance company. Adjustors have a great ability at taking plenty of time, yet the small businessman, or homeowner, cannot wait. You have to settle promptly. The adjustor knows this, and by stalling (using red tape frequently as an excuse), he knows how to win. You lose. He is very capable of interpreting the "fine print." He should be, since the company lawyers have coached him for years.

Life Insurance

Life insurance companies also have it made. How can they lose? Inflation pumps money into their coffers at one end. You and I pump more in at the other end. We are living longer. The only way you can win is to die! The statistics on longevity are relatively easy for them to figure. They base their business on these and the fact that medical science is keeping people alive longer. It is elementary that they cannot lose—but we should realize what is going on in order to buy life insurance properly.

How to Buy Insurance

Big insurance companies take advantage of small business. For example:

Do the large companies pay the same rates that you and I do? Figure it out for yourself. Do you give the same price to a small customer as you do to a large one? Of course you don't. While insurance companies get huge and we stay small (at the same time helping them become larger), we must be wary in our dealings with them. Some suggestions follow.

1. Buy insurance like you buy anything else, whether

raw materials, inventory, labor, or other services. Put your insurance out for bids. Insurance agents are a dime a dozen in any community—let them compete for your business. Let each one give his pitch. You will be surprised how they will differ. Then you decide.

2. Forget the "friendly agent" who makes the point that he is a member of your club. Many insurance problems are our own fault because we buy insurance on the basis of friendship. Far too much insurance business is awarded for this reason. It is difficult to be businesslike with friends, especially when the odds are against you, as they are with insurance. The only way you can win is to lose!

3. When you give your insurance business to an agent, don't make it a marriage. Consider changing every two or three years. Get new bids. Let your agent bid only if he has served you well. If no one else offers better coverage at lower prices, or can *guarantee* better service, it is probably better to stick with your agent. Taking bids from his competitors will keep him on his toes. Let him know it.

Even if your agent keeps your business several years, it is still wise to get other bids every so often. Never stop. Insurance companies and laws cause frequent changes.

4. In buying material which you either convert to your product or resell, you would not think of having only one source of supply. Buying insurance is no different. Each time a "friendly agent" calls on you, or you request bids, ask him to take a survey of your requirements. Let him see the policies you now have. Maybe he will come up with a better deal for you. If not, you have the benefit of an objective opinion of your coverage.

Is this disloyal? No, it is just plain good business. Your old "friendly agent" cannot possibly (or does not) get around to visit his customers often enough. This is not your fault, so feel free to help competition take its course. You do in everything else you buy without giving it a second thought. Insurance agents have built a mystique that they are your close advisors and special pals. Many small businessmen fall for it and feel disloyal about even discussing the subject with another agent.

Letting personalities enter your business is not professional. A better plan is to split your coverage between agents, if you can do it without paying extra. Let one have your fire insurance, for instance, and another have your workmen's compensation. This keeps you in contact with at least two agents.

5. By all means split up your life insurance and your liability and casualty coverage. Though some agents consider themselves experts in both lines, most insurance professionals admit that to really service his clientele, an agent must concentrate on one or the other. Health insurance is a field by itself, with agents who specialize in nothing else.

If you let one agent, or agency, handle both life and liability, you can expect less service. The agent may tell you that by buying everything from him you will be a large enough customer to merit more of his time. In practice, this seldom works out. If two agents are handling your policies you will get twice the service. You short-change yourself in advice also. Two agents' ideas are better than one.

If you provide health and accident insurance as a fringe benefit, or buy a group policy so employees (and yourself) can get the lower rates, let a third agent who specializes in that type of coverage handle it or at least bid on it.

6. Insurance professionals are specialists, just as you specialize as a professional businessman. This eliminates the part-time agent from any consideration. Forget him.

The only reason you would consider him is friendship, which is both unprofessional and expensive.

The real professional is a life insurance agent who has studied and met other requirements for his Certified Life Underwriter (CLU) designation, and the casualty agent who has met similar standards in his field and been awarded Certified Liability and Casualty Underwriter (CLCU) designation. They have pledged themselves to a strict professional code of ethics. They can be expelled for violations, and this is an added protection to you.

They are highly respected by their companies and can better represent you with them. They know the angles. Often they are the ones who work out new angles. If you possibly can, have your insurance handled by CLUs and CLCUs.

7. Buy insurance, especially life insurance, from mutual companies. A mutual insurance company is owned by its policyholders. Instead of paying out its profits to stockholders, they are given back to the policyholders.

A stock company probably cannot give as good a deal since it must pay dividends. This may not always be true. The lowest cost insurance is provided by the company with the lowest operating cost. Money wasted in operations cannot be returned in dividends, whether the company is mutual or stock. Complete company and industry statistics are available from your agent. Ask them what their company's operating costs are and how they compare with the industry. Their financial statements should be provided.

Purchasing Professional Services

Special purchasing problems that warrant further mention have to do with using the services of the professions.

Professional vendors make you think they are vastly different and far more important. That is just their sales pitch. Don't fall for it. If you do you will find yourself paying more than they are worth to you.

What professional vendors are required by small business? There are four: lawyers, accountants, insurance men, and public relations and advertising practitioners. Most small businesses do not require the services of the "world's oldest profession," but if you should, it would be easier to determine if you are getting your money's worth than with most of the others.

These suppliers are alike except they offer intangibles rather than the materials you buy from other vendors. The need for them, however, is just as important as for pencils or cash registers. The difference is that, most of their services being intangible, it is harder to know what is a fair price. Pencils have a going rate which you can easily check.

When you request advice or services from a professional, neither he nor you knows how much it will cost. Therefore, he cannot quote an exact price the way the pencil-seller does. In his years of acquiring a specialized education, the professional must place high rates on his services to recoup his investment. Few of the cases he handles are *exactly* alike. Your particular case may require extra time because you ask many questions. It is important for you to get these answers, but your professional has only time to sell and has to charge for it, and it is not possible to measure the results accurately. You cannot be sure the consultation time your lawyer billed for is accurate unless you carry a time clock and have him punch in and out.

As a result, you have to be doubly cautious in dealing

with your professional vendors. First, select the best one for you. Interview him as you would any other vendor (except, perhaps, be a little more discreet). Second, see that you are charged only for the time used in your behalf. Third, insure that you get full value.

Most professional vendors tend to hold themselves and their position in high esteem. It is easy to be awed by them. But don't avoid using their services. One small businessman I know indignantly claims he will use a lawyer only to sue someone or if he is being sued. That is an ostrich attitude. With all the laws under which business operates today, you cannot get along without lawyers. You may not find it easy to get along *with* them either.

Expenditures on professional services must be kept in proportion, because they usually offer only negative assistance. They protect and conserve but seldom expand your business—advertising and engineering excepted.

I have often thought that we small businessmen should *change* our professional vendors occasionally.

Lawyers. It is hard to switch attorneys since he is the one that probably helped set up your company, at least in its legal form. That is one reason a change may be healthy. You feel you are stuck with him . . . and he knows it. A switch will get you a newly objective look at your organization. If you have grown, or made changes, the new attorney can probably offer some positive suggestions. He cannot advertise, so once you call him he may do his utmost to help you.

If you are stuck with your present lawyer for some reason, there is nothing to prevent you from talking (off the record, perhaps) with other attorneys. Consult them about your problems. Since you are most likely one of his smaller clients, the chances are your lawyer is asleep.

There is no law that says you cannot switch lawyers. Don't worry about papers he has in his files or confidential information you have given him. Professional ethics dictate that he keep quiet about the latter and make available the former to your new lawyer *on your request*. Or you can ask him outright to return your records. Remember, he is just another vendor. You would not hesitate to ask a parts subcontractor to return *your* blueprints.

Accountants and auditors. Since you are probably one of their smaller accounts, you may not be getting their best talent or abilities. At least you usually do not after you have been with them awhile and your account has become routine. By changing to a new firm you can command top men, at least while you are a "new" client. They, nearly always, can show you improvements you should have made before.

Advertising agencies. Again, as a small account, it is doubtful that the best men are assigned to your work. A new agency trying to win your account will try harder, at least in the beginning. In most situations it makes sense to change agencies every two or three years.

Liability insurance underwriters. Unless your community is very small, so that there may not be much choice, this supplier may need changing as often as every other year. The room for savings in liability insurance in most states is great. You may lose a few "friends" by changing, but you will save lots of money.

Life insurance agents. More loyalty is due this vendor. Since he is handling types of insurance which require much planning—key man, pensions, your own life insurance—he must grow with your company. Even if you change agents, it may be unwise to change companies (except on term insurance). That requires canceling policies and replacing them with new ones, which may mean losing cash values and having to pay higher premiums. Within the insurance company you may request a change of agents, but the original one still gets renewal commissions on your policies so you are not really rid of him.

Under these circumstances make sure he calls on you regularly, and that he comes to you with suggestions to keep your policies and insurance plans up-to-date. He gets his commissions on your business every year. Make him earn it by giving you service.

If he is on the ball he will look after your affairs well, because that will provide him opportunities to sell you more insurance.

In practice it may be difficult to change professional vendors often, or at all. But don't feel you are stuck with any of them. You are not, not any more than with any supplier or employee.

One word of caution: Don't change professionals unless, or until, you are completely paid up. If you make a change while owing them they can hurt you in the community. They have their grapevine, just as the bankers, and can quickly pass around the word to their fellow professionals that you are no-pay or slow-pay (which, being small, you may be).

The thing to look for in a professional is his knowledge of small business. By training and orientation the great majority of them simply are not equipped to serve small business. Large commercial law firms want the big business clients. The law schools orient their courses to serve the big companies.

Accountants like to work on complicated and intricate financial situations. It is only natural, as these are more challenging to their ingenuity and training. Most advertising agencies still operate on an outmoded commission system. The more you spend, the more they make. Naturally their interest is in the big spenders. Insurance agents may be more small-business-oriented, since the big companies often deal directly with the home office at lower rates. Even so, an agent will naturally pick a larger client over you if he has the choice.

To really help you, and to be able to apply the latest developments in his field to your problems, the professional must have a solid understanding of small business. Yet few members of the professions do. Ironically, their own practices are small business . . . merely in a highly specialized field.

PART THREE

MANAGEMENT TIPS

CHAPTER X

Big Frog, Little Pond

ALL business starts with a sale. But in many small companies it may not be a profitable sale. And instead of building a carefully planned market position, this—and every other sale—may be simply catch-as-catch-can.

This is the difference between medieval peddling and modern marketing.

Marketing is not just business school jargon. It is the control system that makes sales easier and more profitable. It is a road map directing you to your customers.

It begins in research and takes shape with forecasts based on its findings. It then gets sellers together with buyers, supply tied into demand. At its highest level, marketing attempts to discover an entire nation's needs and availabilities—or perhaps the world's.

One such resource is *The Statistical Abstract of the United States*, which is issued every year by the Government Printing Office. It sounds like a tome, and it is. But taking some time to leaf through this massive volume of statistics can give you important information about your own small business.

For example, you can find out in this book not only that the projected population of the United States in the sources those people are likely to need. For example, the year 2000 is 267,000,000 people, but what kinds of re-

government projects the need for every type of metals, for
plastics, even for recreation equipment. These projections
might well affect your planning and sales.

Don't think marketing is mere jargon. It is talking to—
and about—you, Mr. Small Business Man. As you become more adept at marketing and marketing research,
you will probably agree that there is one simple but essential rule for small business success:

> *Choose a small market and develop it until you domi-
> nate. Be a big frog in a small pond.*

Pick one in which big business is not interested. They are
vicious competitors. Why fight them, when there are hundreds of markets they cannot touch?

If you happen to be in a market which competes with
big business, move to a smaller segment of that market.
Volkswagen in the U.S. has done all right despite the most
rugged competition. Big companies can survive only on
tremendous volume. This opens up the market for specialized lesser-volume products to small business.

Ours is such a huge country that even though your
segment of a market may be very narrow, it still has room
for your company to grow to a sizable business.

Let Water Seek Its Own Level

A specific study of your market is not difficult to com-
pile whether you run a grocery store or a nationally
branded manufacturing company. A welter of statistics are
generated by government and private sources. All you
need do is cull the ones which refer to you. SBA and state
university departments are available to help you do so.

Market data are collected in monumental quantities by several levels of government, trade, and industry associations, independent research groups, and individual businesses. Surprisingly, in view of the varied sources, it is available in relatively unconflicting patterns. Enough different sources exist so that most statistics can be cross-checked.

This can be valuable to the small businessman who has no research staff of his own. It should indicate good chances for success, not only for the locality but for the industry.

The same incisive probing of the market that is done before big business launches a new product should precede starting a new business. In addition to gathering statistical data, the community should be checked carefully. Even though what they tell you will probably be based on stereotyped thinking, the opinions of those in a position to know should be gotten, such as bankers and Chamber of Commerce officials. They may contain warnings or leads for fruitful inquiry.

Certainly the competition needs checking. Are they successful? Planning to expand themselves? It is a good idea also to be sure they are not planning to sell out soon. You may be able to buy your way into the market or decide to open your own company sooner than projected in order to force down the price at which you can later buy the competitor.

Dun & Bradstreet and other credit reports indicate what the business community thinks of your competitors in terms of what credit they command. To get really inside information, hire a private detective. Industrial espionage is currently a moral crisis within a big business, and this is by no means a suggestion that the affair be carried that far. It may be more efficient to hire a professional investigator to ferret out hard-core confidential data than to go snooping around yourself, except for openly questioning bankers, friends, and other known sources.

However it is done, facts must be gathered. Opening businesses on intuition or hunch is one of the rules that have changed. Most small companies today are founded on some research and statistics. If you have doubts, they will be quickly erased when you ask the bank to loan money for your new venture.

What Type Community Should You Choose for a New Business?

If you have a choice, should you pick a growing town or a decadent one? There are good points on both sides. There may not be as much opportunity for small business in a growing community as in a retarded one. A few small companies can start a backward community growing again. Franchises, for example, may already be taken in a growing area but available in a decadent one.

Small businesses help small communities thrive. If you are considering starting one, here are a few things to think about.

In small communities there are two kinds of businesses: one which obtains its income primarily from within the community, and the other which obtains its income from the outside.

There are still many economically backward communities in the United States. Check the population growth in the last 25 to 50 years in yours. Some New England towns and cities, for example, still have the same population as they did 100 years ago. Would this area be a good one in which to start a new business? Actually it might be the best or it could be the worst! If considerable amount of your sales income is going to come from outside the area, it might be the best. The town fathers have been struggling for years to obtain new business. The banks today, even the most unprogressive, can be convinced to help. There is usually a good labor force available, and they will be sincere in trying to better themselves and your company.

A stagnant community provides other more subtle opportunities for you. The people there provide less competition because of the slower pace. It isn't that they are not as smart but rather they do not have the drive that you might have, coming from a large area. If you are successful, you may be the most unpopular guy in town because you will have perhaps demonstrated what they could have done themselves. However, you did not move there to win a popularity contest, or run for mayor. You moved, or started a new business there, because it was a good business decision.

If your new business is a service-type business and depends wholly for its sales (income) from *within* the community, you had better take another look. A new concern doing business locally *only*, in an old, unprogressive city or town, may have tough sledding. Even if your service is better, it might take years before you will be accepted. You can easily end up becoming one of a large group who have been ekeing out a small living for years in a "cornered" market.

Someone once said that "opportunity exists in direct ratio to the ability to be of service." In that sense there is actually greater opportunity in a town which is not presently growing. But investigate it carefully before you take the plunge.

Another consideration of small business is the importance of not merely *taking in each other's washing*. Get into a business which is not dependent on friends and neighbors. Such a company adds nothing to the town (unless the service is not otherwise available). To make your town grow, you should be "export-import minded." That is, you should sell your goods out of town in order to bring *new* money in. If your company does business only within the town, the same dollars are going round and round.

Types of Small Business Available

All business can be divided into manufacturing (including construction), distribution or sales, and services. Within these broad categories, the Standard Industrial Classification Code lists 901 specific types of enterprise! Our economy is so vast it provides for many products and services. This is another way in which opportunity abounds.

Which business category is both right for and brimming with reasonably rapid success? That requires a personal answer. If correctly formulated, it will be based on intense self-study and extensive market research. Some suggestions on various small businesses may help guide you.

Manufacturing

Since capital gains offer the greatest opportunity for wealth, their potential is the foremost consideration of any business. On this basis, manufacturing by and large has more to offer than other fields—provided you have the sales.

There are two types of manufacturing delineated by their sales methods. Proprietary manufacturers produce a product of their own, usually marketing it themselves. Contract manufacturers, or job shops, produce other companies' products for them, in whole or in part. Job shops are more service businesses than manufacturers, since they exist at the whim of other manufacturers to service their needs. When the Jiffy Whatzit needs gizzards, Johnson's Metal Company may be asked to produce them. And it may not if some other job shop has gotten to Jiffy's management with a lower price. Price competition in such a narrow market can be brutal. If Johnson's is slated for the order, they will not get it until and unless Jiffy's sales of Whatzits calls for a new production run.

Job shops have no control over the ultimate consumption of the final end product. This is a serious weakness.

Avoidance of marketing is what prompts most job shop owners to enter this type of manufacturing. As a group, they are artisans who know foundries, or machining, or plastics, intimately—but have little confidence in their own sales ability. Their specialized knowledge might appeal to other manufacturers, however, so that is where they look for orders. Because of this independent position for sales, contract manufacturing is an up-and-down business—feast or famine. Because competition in most areas is fierce, profit margins are low.

To take a random example, Robert Morris Associates' *Statement Studies* for 1966 shows gross profits in small business, nonferrous foundries (largely a job shop industry) to average 14%, with net profits averaging 1¾%. Small cutlery and hand tools manufacturing, which produce proprietary goods, have gross profits averaging 29%, with a net of 3½%. Though this is a random sample, it is interesting to note that the hand tool industry is highly competitive, controlled by giants, and suffering from imports.

The know-how is in the manufacturing, but success is in the marketing. Manufacturing requires a management team. One man can operate a retail or service business alone or with few helpers. Very few manufacturing businesses can be run by one man today.

· A trend among proprietary manufacturers is toward becoming essentially assembly plants. Components are bought from specialty producers, or job shops, then assembled and marketed by the manufacturer. Often subassemblies are purchased outside so that only final assembly is done by the company which owns the product. This is possible because the important thing is *selling* the product, not *making* it. It is easier to make it than to sell it!

General Motors' ability to market automobiles is many times more important than all its plant and equipment and even its production know-how. If it could not sell the cars, it would not have to bother making them. This is an oversimplification, to be sure, but an important guideline for the small businessman starting a new company.

Some "manufacturers" do no manufacturing. They own the product and market it but contract its entire production with a job shop. New products are often launched this way, to conserve capital. Or to release all capital for the important thing successfully establishing the product in the market. Often such companies take over manufacturing when it becomes expedient for them to do so. Which means that the job shop which had a fat contract to produce a complete product is once again looking for work.

Frequently manufacturing companies reverse this trend and begin as job shops. This is usually because the skills of management are primarily in production; the job shop route is used to get a company established and financed. From the beginning the object is to find, or invent, proprietary products which the company will ultimately control and market. If this helps you get started, okay. But only for a start. Until a product is found, there is little capital gains potential to speak of in job shop manufacturing companies.

Manufacturing is the most difficult of all businesses because it is really an amalgam of several businesses: raw material, acquisition, productions, financing, product design, marketing. Each of these constitutes separate business entities. It is also the most rewarding business.

Finding the right product and product mix, whether a new one or a variation on an existing product, is the key.

One other marketing factor no business can overlook, large or small, is pricing.

Pricing Is Profit

Remember the story about the guy who lost money on every item but made it up on volume? Or the cartoon showing the bum telling one of his fellow hoboes, "I was always the low bidder"?

Many small businesses are afraid to charge enough for their products or service. In order to get the sale, sales managers frequently would give it away.

Too often we do not value our own services highly enough because we are too close to them. Whatever the reason, many small businessmen base their prices on what the market will bear without strong sales effort. It is that extra selling that can enable you to command the extra profit.

A fair price is one that includes a reasonable profit. Customers naturally look for bargains, but most of them know you cannot get something for nothing. They are willing to pay a fair price but they have to be convinced.

In order to make a profit *you* must set the prices—not your sales manager or your customer. How can he set a price that will allow you a profit when he doesn't know what your costs are?

Fear of charging enough may be lack of self-confidence. Perhaps it results from lack of confidence in the quality of your merchandise or service. If so, you had better switch brands or, if a manufacturer, greatly improve your product. If *you* don't have confidence in it, who will?

Or it may be the result of strong competitive pressure. If the company down the street can sell for less than you, there must be a reason. The place to begin fighting such competition is to *find out* the reason. That is where we usually fail. Instead of coolly investigating to find the cause of lower-priced competition, we panic.

If your competitor charges less, making little or no profit at all, you may have to drop near his level for a while. Only long enough to start outselling him, however. Or perhaps he is more desperate than you are; going broke sooner. Wait and see.

It is true that you usually get what you pay for. Therefore, in most instances, you have a ready competitive answer to lower prices; you can get more if you give more. Keep selling.

Giant discounters can underprice small retailers on the exact same brand of goods. There is little you can do about that—or is there?

You can emphasize your smallness, including the first-name friendliness and service that go with it. Coupled with these is the fact you personally stand behind your merchandise—to make repairs, replacements, adjustments. You have got to do this when you are a small, friendly business. The giant discounter often will not—or cannot.

Whatever your competitive situation, there is something in your favor. You can compete with almost anyone. You can be friendlier, more convenient, give more personal service, handle different lines, or offer something special besides just price.

When you analyze it, high price is far from a disadvantage. In bad times the carriage trade always seems to survive.

The low-markup, volume outfit is usually in trouble. Its reputation and market have been built strictly on price. When that advantage is wiped out, so may the company.

If you have a choice between price or quality, take quality. It has always been true that with some sales effort most people will buy quality.

Don't Try to Make It Cheaper!

In the long run a lower cost has to be the result of volume. Small business practitioners are kidding themselves if they try to compete on price.

Frequently you hear someone say, when discussing some new product idea for his small business, "We can sell a million of these!" But he can't really. He doesn't have the capital to move that kind of volume. If he could get it, it would mean changing the nature of his company to handle such business. He doesn't have the distribution or sales either. The company would end up without the advantages and protections of big business. It would be vulnerable to competition from all quarters—and nine chances out of ten it would soon be swallowed up by a corporate giant, or simply be put out of its misery.

Perhaps the owner would realize a fortune from this and be happy to retire and forget business. But, if he is a professional small businessman, he would not want to retire in any case. He would have to go out and start again.

If you are determined to be a big frog in a big pond, small business may not be for you. But big business may not be either. How few of the men who enter giant corporations attain positions of such responsibility that they are really running things? Most end up being small frogs in a big pond.

What if your personality or interests are not geared to a low-volume, high-quality, special-service operation, although you have all the attributes of the small business pro? Perhaps a franchise is your answer, where you are able to offer relatively low prices and attain relatively high volume as the local outlet of a national brand.

Pricing to the market is one lesson small business can learn from big business. The battery of economists, market researchers, statisticians, and computers used by a big business to arrive at the proper market price would easily exceed the total staff and investment of a large number of small companies.

But even that great advantage does not enable big business to eliminate smaller competitors. Because of its size, big business must produce in volume and peg its prices to appeal to the mass market.

There is always plenty of room for the specialized or quality small company to fill in at higher price levels.

Pricing Means Cost Accounting

Cost accounting is another technique small businessmen should borrow from big business. Accountants report that the majority of small businesses operate only on profit-loss bookkeeping without regard to profit-loss accounting by item or product line.

Cost accounting is important. It tells which activities to carry on and which to discontinue—which are profitable and which are not.

Everyone knows what his own discount or markup is. But a surprising number of businessmen have no conception of the overall breakdown of a product's selling price.

If materials used in the manufacture of an item cost $30, direct labor for its production might cost $10, or a total of $40 for labor and materials to produce a single unit.

Direct labor overhead runs from 60 to 120% and could easily equal the cost of labor and materials, doubling the cost to $80. General and administrative overhead, including accounting, supervision, sales management, etcetera, may run 20 to 30%. Thus, a product whose materials cost $30 has an overall cost of around $96—*before* profit is added. If you attempt to make a profit of 20%, the unit's total cost, on the shipping dock, has reached $116.

Direct cost of sales must then be added. In the traditional method of distribution, by which a sales agent sells to a distributor or wholesaler, who, in turn, sells to the retailer, a percentage for each must be included. Sales reps up to 10%, distributors up to 30%, and retailers up to 50% markup.

(Although cost accounting is computed by the markup method, salesmen usually present the products by the discount. This adds more confusion to pricing.)

Set standards of markups, commissions and discounts have broken down in recent years, even with single industries. Those quoted here are for higher price product lines. Lower price items often carry 100% markup or higher. If the retailer pays $.25, sometimes he sells for $.50.

The point is that the manufacturer's profit, as well as the profit of each level of distribution, has been carefully computed into the retail selling price. If you do not do likewise with every item you make or handle, and with every service you offer, chances are very good you may be working for nothing. If you are a manufacturer, it is quite normal for your customers, distributors, and dealers to be making more on your product than you are.

Your Business and Your Competitors

Assume you are a successful small businessman who has gained a certain share of your market. You are doing well but are not satisfied. Growth is what you are after.

Be careful from where you get your growth!

Don't try too hard to unbalance the existing market situation. For example, four companies share a market on this basis:

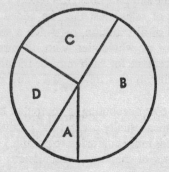

Company B attempts to move in on C and D's business. This usually makes them fight that much harder, knowing their market share is being invaded. C and D might gang up on B and lick him.

Or B might try to obtain some of little A's volume. But A was one of the pioneers of the product. He helped create the market they all share now. Probably some owners and executives of the other competitors once worked for A, perhaps learned the business from him. C and D could have knocked A out years ago. But he is a nice guy, the elder statesman of the industry. So they have left him alone with his little share of the market. If B goes after A, then A, C, and D will clobber him.

Or perhaps A's share is a highly specialized one, in product or price, which he can serve profitably because he is geared to it—but which would be a nuisance to the other companies if they had to work it into their lines. It is better for them to have A around.

If B tackles D's major market he may be biting off more than he can chew, financially, production-wise, in sales staffing, etcetera.

Conclusion: Do not rock the competitive boat too much in a stable market, where each company is operating profitably and deserving the business it has.

How Can Company B Grow?

It can grow by helping the market grow. This is better for everyone. Get your major growth out of market growth rather than taking business from competitors. That is a vicious circle. You take a few accounts away from them, they take some away from you. Soon, all the competitors are doing is swapping accounts. Sales costs and emotions run high. Everybody in the industry is so concentrated on this game of customer roulette they do not notice a new little company, E, is introducing an improved product. And frequently E is a former employee.

Now all the competitors frantically tool up to make their product competitive with the improved newcomer. Such forced product change is expensive. It has ruined more than one small business, and a few big ones.

It is better to leave market balance alone, by and large. More understanding is needed among small business competitors. It is senseless for small companies to fight among themselves when they have enough battle on their hands with all their other problems. It is common knowledge that big business has tacit agreements about market shares.

Small business operators are not professional enough about this. They usually hate their competitors' guts and will not even talk with them. This permits emotion to supersede good judgment.

It overlooks the potent factor of inter-industry competition. When an industry becomes absorbed in fighting within itself over customers and market shares, it takes its eyes off the goal of industry growth which can best be achieved by customer-oriented rather than competition-oriented marketing.

Sales Reps vs. Sales Force

The other side of marketing is selling. Advertising can do some of it for you. In a few businesses, such as direct mail, advertising must do it all. In most companies it is actual personal sales contacts that carry out the marketing program.

Should the individuals who do your company selling be employees? Or commission agents?

Manufacturers have lived with this problem for a long time. Each system has its advantages. Most big companies have done away with reps.

Initially reps are hired by companies because they add little overhead, since they are paid only on sales they bring in. The system has enabled countless small business product lines to be sold nationally.

Many a small company simply cannot afford its own sales force. It is stuck with reps. This economic factor must have priority consideration. But there are dangers too.

Reps are altogether too powerful for the good of some of the small companies they represent. Because they are the source of a company's orders they wield power. By turning over such a vital aspect of your business as sales to an outside group, you leave your company extremely vulnerable.

There have been many incidents of smoke-filled convention room confabs at 1 A.M. where a company's reps gather to decide whether they will attempt to have so-and-so fired as sales manager. Because they control sales, reps come to feel they should decide company policy, prices, personnel, and other issues. Reps seldom take any credit responsibility. You take all the credit risk.

Sales reps usually try to keep their manufacturers separated from their customers, and vice versa. Manufacturers with reps are frequently in the position of having no relationship with the persons and companies whose orders are keeping them in business.

Remember also that reps' interests are not fully tied up to yours. Reps have other lines too. Yours probably is not their major line. Some representatives have 50 to 100 different product lines competing with you for their sales efforts.

The investment in sales *samples* for a string of reps covering the nation can be high. This burden falls completely on you.

A new company or product must start with the "dog" reps—the new or incapable ones. But as soon as a dog rep becomes successful, he weeds out his small original lines —maybe yours—and looks for greener pastures. Most representative contract arrangements can be canceled by either party upon 30 to 60 days' notice.

On the other hand, if you can attract top reps, the guys known throughout the industry and with fine reputations, you may be no better off. They have lived off the fat of their lines so long as order takers, they have forgotten how to sell. They are buddies with all their customers and that is how they move merchandise. Let a problem or situation requiring salesmanship come along and they are likely to represent the customer rather than you, or worse, concentrate on their other lines.

For new companies or products they are particularly dangerous. Their customers buy on the word of these reps. Therefore, the customer has not really been sold. How can *he* then sell the item to his customers? The answer is he can't, so he drops your line. You have paid the rep's commission and he has quit; back for credit comes a load of stuff he "sold," and guess who is left holding the bag.

To their credit, reps were once the sales lifeline of industry. But old-time reps, like old-time bankers, are things of the past. Some pro reps are still around.

Hiring Salesmen

Perhaps more has been written on sales techniques and managing salesmen than any other commercial topic.

Most of it is logical. Much of it is entertaining reading, full of success tales and brilliant selling tricks.

One technique on how to find and hire good salesmen is to hire salesmen who call on you. It locates men who are already in selling and who might not answer a sales help-wanted ad. You have the opportunity to look them over and actually watch them in action from the other side of the desk.

If you run an ad for sales help, avoid giving it a "we want" slant. Substitute a "we have an unusual opportunity for" approach. In the ad prospective salesmen want to know what you can do for them. Just as in the interview good prospects will concentrate on telling what they believe they can do for you.

A really good salesman is hard to find. You may have to overlook some things in hiring him. Give him a chance for a limited time (that you both agree on) and don't hesitate to fire him at the right time.

Here are a few "don't hire" suggestions:

> If applicant has had too many jobs in the last five years —two is OK but three or more is questionable—he may be a floater
> If an applicant has gaps between jobs
> If he has had a recent business failure
> If an applicant has no selling experience
> If an applicant has made no upward salary progress in his last job or from job to job

The above "don't hire" rules are very general. These questions ought to be asked, certainly. But there may be legitimate answers. Notice how well he sells you with his answers. It is possible a prospect on this list might be a good one for your sales force. If you play it too safe, you may get lackluster salesmen who may be steady but barely earn their keep.

Rather than being dogmatic in hiring procedure, let new salesmen know they are on trial for the first six months to a year. To check on them, reask the questions at a later date. Did the answers stay the same?

Check the new man's progress at ninety days. In that time if he is not performing at half of what is ultimately expected of him, consider dropping him.

Pioneering New Products

While we are on the subject of marketing and marketable products, let's talk about one source of them, the inventor. Nearly every businessman, at some time in his life, comes up with an idea for a product. Ask anyone.

The market has grown so huge and so gadget-conscious that your idea probably is a good one, perhaps even marketable. So what? Everyone has product ideas but how many—even those that become everyday household objects—ever become profitable to the inventor? Besides, you cannot patent an idea!

The courts, in recent times, have done little to protect the inventor. The confused state of patent law and its enforcement are mainly responsible and most inventors die broke. Congress has been talking about a patent law revision and may enact one. Until it does, the position of the individual inventor is difficult.

Probably 90% of all product ideas are gadgets. They will never achieve general usage, but may be great mail order or specialty items. The remaining 10% are fundamental inventive improvements, for which the need is tremendous—and the perils great. First of all, to manufacture his own product of this type, immense financing is needed by the inventor. He may find a partner or group of stockholders with money and be able to pull through. Even if he does, he will probably do better financially if he plans to sell out later for the capital gain.

If the inventor of a fundamental improvement takes it to an established manufacturer, he must go through a discouraging round of inquiry and investigation of himself and his idea. Waiting rooms are crowded with others like him.

If and when a company shows real interest in purchasing an item, royalties are usually the goal of the inventor. Considering the mortality rate of even the most sophisticated products, this may be a mistake, because product ideas and improvements multiply so rapidly.

More beneficial is an arrangement whereby the purchaser contracts to hire the inventor as consultant for a specified period at set duties and salary. Beyond that period royalties may be specified, in the unlikely event the idea is still usable. This saves taxes, since the income is spread over several years, enabling the inventor to use the income to start another business, like a truly professional small businessman.

Occasionally manufacturers are willing to buy a product idea outright. Even then it is better to arrange the deal so that payment comes over an extended period.

Don't be fooled by the popular impression that all inventions are made by teams of white-coated scientists working in the clean-room atmosphere of a giant corporation's laboratories. The White House Committee on Small

Business reported that of 61 fundamental inventions of the twentieth century, more than half were by individual inventors working on their own.

The problem is not coming up with a good idea. It is the complex challenge of producing and marketing it.

The general counsel of the Small Business Administration isolated the problem in a speech to the New York Patent Law Association. Philip Zeidman told the patent bar:

> Most conventional sources of private financing are restrained by either law or a self-imposed reluctance to expose their resources to the risks entailed in assisting exploitation of the new ideas developed by independent inventors and small concerns.

He went on to show how shortsighted this attitude is, citing the success of companies formed expressly to make risk investments, like the Rockefeller Brothers, J. H. Whitney & Co., and American Research & Development Corporation. The latter's portfolio at the end of 1965, said Zeidman, "included investments in 43 companies valued at $42.5 million, which has cost ARDC $14 million—proof that risk investments can and are being made and made successfully."

Although there is a surprising number of full-time inventors—385,000, according to the Patent, Trademark and Copyright Institute of George Washington University —it would be inaccurate to call them small businessmen. They are artists or scientists. We are concerned with small businessmen who seek to branch out by exploiting their own product ideas and are not planning to make inventing a career. If you need a product to manufacture and market, why not find an appropriate inventor? Give him some stock and encouragement and get him on your team.

On the other hand, if you are already in business, new products can frequently expand your horizons. Ideas that utilize your existing production and marketing facilities, without overtaxing your financing, have the finest growth potential of all.

If you have created the right image, your manufacturing company may attract a steady procession of "inventors" with brown paper bags.

Make a few things clear to the inventor before he opens the bag:

> You may simultaneously have developed the same thing he has, and he must be prepared to take your word for this.

> Is this item patented? (Most big companies will not even talk or look without this, as it avoids lawsuits.)

> You may consider royalty arrangement but likely buy the idea or product outright if you want it. (Whatever product you make it may be copied. So do not get caught with an inflexible royalty which may keep you from adjusting price to meet competition.)

> If you should buy this item, you should only do it on a "consulting" deal whereby the inventor receives monthly fees. (Fees are deductible. If a company buys a product per se, it must capitalize it—which has tax and other financial disadvantages.) Besides, it is a good idea to have the inventor around for a while to help make the production model work as well as his proto-type. If it does not, you can stop the fee.

While you might be lucky and have a newly developed product walk in your door, chances are greater you will have to develop and improve it yourself. It is a long, costly road from a working model to the finished product, tested and ready to be sold.

New products which are not compatible with your present product line are dangerous. If you have ample capital to develop such an item then create a separate division of your company for it. Or use it to start Company No. 2.

The noteworthy feature of new product pioneering is its cost in both *money* and *time*. Small business pros budget both on the conservative side. If you are sure your new product will be perfected and ready for testing in six months, give yourself eight. If you are sure the item will be ready for production in three months, allow six. You are certain it will then be ready to ship in sixty days, so allow 120. But don't let anyone else know.

Include additional time for market testing.

Cost of pioneering new products is not limited to the manufacturer. Retailers must prepare for problems too. First, your sales staff will have to become familiar with it in order to sell it. Secondly, you can count on complaints because of bugs in the product or customer misunderstanding of how the product operates or exactly what it will and will not do. Finally, because it is unknown, you may have to spend extra promotional funds.

For manufacturers, cost of patent protection can be considerable. Most patents are not worth it. Continual outlays must be made to protect them from infringement. This requires additional patents to protect the original.

Patents have a life of 17 years. At the current speed of technology most are obsolete before they expire.

Developing the product is only the beginning. Dr. Land, inventor of the Polaroid camera, puts forth the rule of thumb that for every dollar of research on a new product there must be ten dollars invested in development and one hundred dollars in production and marketing.

The first production run of a new product seldom shows a profit. Then it has to be sold. Every buyer wants to see the item, mostly from curiosity. Usually only the smaller, riskier customers will order. The big ones want to "check and wait." Every new product has bugs in it which customers are anxious to find, as if it were a treasure hunt. When they find them, they are considered *reasons not to pay you.*

This means you should allow an unusually high reserve for bad debts for the first year or two. This must be included in your original estimated budget.

Failure of new products in the marketplace is one of the phenomena of life in the second half of this century. The average supermarket is estimated to stock 8,000 food and 5,000 nonfood items—of which 1,000 did not exist one year earlier. New product mortality is high.

A Boston specialist in new food products estimates only 5% of the new or "improved" products marketed last year are around today. Lack of promotion and sales eliminates perhaps a quarter of them. But the rest die of simple product inferiority.

Small business cannot afford to launch many new products that do not succeed. Product and market research may be cheap compared with losing your business because a new product failed.

Is pioneering a new product worth such obstacles?

Professor Arnold C. Krannert of Purdue conducted a study of this question, then published an article titled, "Small Companies Can Pioneer New Products" in the *Harvard Business Review.*

Professor Krannert concluded that the risk was very high. His article documents several aspects of the problem. But he counters with this factor:

*At the same time, there are also risks in other kinds of
business activity, just as there are elements of risk in
doing nothing or in hoping that a competitor will miss
an opportunity to make your product obsolete.*

Do not try to design and build the whole new product
just because you happen to have a good idea or a patent
on one part of it. Manufacture your component and sell it
to a larger company that is already in the business. Pick
one whose products *need* your new component. Just because you have developed a new circuit for a TV set is no
reason for going into the manufacturing of complete sets.

This does not mean you become a job shop. You will be
aggressively marketing a component which you control as
your proprietary product.

You will be gearing your business to the essential marketing peculiarities of small business by choosing a narrow
section of the market—and dominating it. Big frog, little
pond.

CHAPTER XI

The Foremost
Executive Skill

WHETHER a company has ten or a thousand employees it cannot expect to function or supervise without a chain of command. There has to be someone to take charge when the owner is absent.

"But," some small business owners retort, "I am always there. I open in the morning and close at night. And I haven't had a vacation in years."

The man who says that—not you, I hope—identifies himself as completely unprofessional. He has fallen in love with his business—or become a slave to it.

More than a chain of command is necessary. Unless yours is literally a one-man operation, division of responsibility is unavoidable. When you hire your first helper the work load must be split up. Incredibly, many small businessmen have not formalized a division of the work to be done.

Within a company of some size, job descriptions are helpful, even an essential tool. They clearly outline for each worker where his responsibilities begin and end.

Management spells success or failure in all things and especially in small business . . . because it has so little room for error. But what exactly is management?

Samuel Feinberg, Fairchild Publications columnist on

the subject, defines it well in his preface to "How Do You Manage?"

Management or leadership—take your choice—is the art of getting things done through people.

Management is leadership. Every human endeavor requires it.

Many men have not learned to manage themselves, let alone others. Feinberg made this clear in one of his columns discussing the retail field. He pointed out that over 65% of family- or individually owned department and specialty stores existing in 1929 have disappeared or been sold to chains. His list of the reasons why is an indictment of business managers who fail to manage themselves.

"Handmaidens of this virtual suicide complex: greed, vanity, stubbornness, smugness, lethargy, and ignorance. Some manifestations of such sins of commission or omission: nepotism, hazy lines of jurisdiction, ineffective top management, wrangling among principal owners, poor communication up and down the line of command, disregard of human values, apathetic executives, and rank-and-file employees, playing the game of 'follow the leader,' unhealthy balance between (product) lines, deterioration of property, fixtures and equipment, and backwardness in expansion."

Dun & Bradstreet confirms this. Lack of management, says "The Failure Record Through 1965," is the overwhelming cause of business failure, accounting for 91.4% of failures. This breaks down as follows:

    9.9%—lack of experience in the line
    18.8%—lack of managerial experience
    21.4%—unbalanced experience
    41.3%—incompetence

D & B relates such lack of management to "inability to avoid conditions which resulted in inadequate sales, heavy operating expenses, receivables difficulties, inventory difficulties, excessive fixed assets, poor location, competitive weakness."

Are you managing your business? Or, like the operators of the companies which created these statistics, is it managing you?

It is easy to spot businessmen who are not managers. Their companies are run according to circumstance, to any and every situation and obstacle which arises. Circumstances are managing them instead of the other way around. The real manager of such companies is J. P. Circumstance.

Everyone has to make adjustments to conditions he cannot control. The question is whether company policy is changed every time a new set of conditions comes along. Thousands of case histories of companies that did this have been studied. The ironic conclusion is that nearly all would have been better off had they stayed on one course. Circumstances themselves change so often and so wantonly that it is not possible to run a business if you are constantly knuckling under to them. You retrace your steps so often your own feet trip you.

If you set the goals and objectives of your business and manage your human and other resources to reach them, regardless of situations which may arise, you are providing management. Dollars, machines, plants, or products do not do business, people do. Human resources are therefore the most important part of every business. It follows that . . .

The foremost executive skill is organizing and operating a management team.

Managing small business is like the almost-lost art of working a team of horses. You pull one rein, then the other, then both together. You move forward, then you back 'em up a little so you can go forward more smoothly again. .

One who knew this rule and profited from it was Andrew Carnegie. On his tombstone are these words:

> Here lies a man
> Who knew how to enlist
> In his service
> Better men than himself

The president of American Management Association has concluded from his experience that management is the development of people, not the direction of things.

More important, how can the small business pro, who is eager to develop several companies, expect to start Company No. 2 until he has organized a team to run No. 1 without him? He must understand management and the team approach as the lifeblood of his profession, for while he is operating his second and third businesses, his other companies will be run by management teams he has developed.

Without a management team, small business operators cannot start other companies. Developing and directing management teams is, therefore, the foremost part of being a small business pro.

Internal Selling

Ability to manage is the world's most valuable skill. Happily, it is a skill more than an ability. It can be learned.

Primary in learning to manage is an understanding of goals and objectives. How to arrive at them. How to separate short-term goals from long-range objectives. How to formulate policy and allocate resources to achieve your objectives.

These things constitute managing—not giving orders or being "the boss."

Another important ingredient is necessary: How to get your employees and associates to feel involved in the policy and objectives so they will work hard alongside you in pursuit of them.

SBA's management research report, entitled "Providing Management Talent for Small Business," uncovers the basic psychology in operating team effort. "Speaking from a social viewpoint," say the Louisiana State University professors who wrote the report, "the small organization offers a sense of belonging that is missing in larger groups; there is a feeling of *esprit de corps* that cannot be duplicated elsewhere."

Even if some of your employees cannot pronounce *esprit de corps*, they will understand why a sales manager told the author, "A small business is both an economic and social system. There is a sense of belonging that is hard to find in a big company. Also, in a small company the job carries with it a title and responsibility which gives the person a sense of prestige that he would lose if he went to a larger company."

You cannot create teamwork by making everyone a vice-president. You can do it by internal selling.

Executives at all levels rarely spend enough time selling their function and policies and plans to other people in the organization. As a result, internal communications and employee relations are often poor in small business.

Big business has specialists who do nothing but work on these problems. If it did not, the computers and auditors would squelch it. Small business professionals have to create their own employee relations, with emphasis on good communications above all.

External sales are sometimes less important to the success and profitability of a business than internal selling. A franchise, for example, can do little about sales since brand-acceptance and even advertising are provided by the parent company. But adept use of internal selling to keep his team operating at peak efficiency and service is vital to the franchise profits.

A company responsible for generating its own sales, such as a small manufacturer, must also do internal selling. Any department can be crippled if internal strife develops.

The most common solution to internal communications is *the staff meeting*. There everyone publicly reports on his own, or his department's, efforts, problems, objectives and success. Largely because big business got them a bad reputation through overuse, meetings have a bad name with some businessmen. This is unfortunate, because there is no substitute for a face-to-face talk between all of the company's management team members at the same time.

Too frequent meetings render them meaningless, while too sparse dates may fail to achieve the purpose. A *weekly* meeting at an established *time*, each week and every week regardless, is a possible solution. If they become a fixture on your company calendar, weekly meetings have a better chance of succeeding. Frequently excuses will come up to avoid weekly meetings. Don't let this happen. It is like going to church—if you miss one Sunday it is easier to miss the next one.

Another suggestion which has worked for some is to make them slightly *formal*, that is, have those in attendance roll their shirt sleeves down and put on their suitcoats (if that is their normal dress).

You, as chief executive, preside from a *prepared agenda*. Hold the session to the agenda as closely as possible. It may be helpful to have the last item on the agenda be proposals for the next week's meeting, thus providing all with a week to think about it.

Try to *resolve each subject* in some way: by assigning someone to take action, appointing one or two to investigate, deciding to seek outside opinion, etcetera. It is important that definite dates to report back be given—and be sure you include the report on that meeting's agenda. Frequently it helps to rotate the chairman and secretary who takes notes, each week. You had better pay attention because soon it is going to be your turn. Your management team will have more respect for a meeting which is conducted regularly in a businesslike manner. This does not mean they have to be phony—only that they have to be taken seriously.

Friction may still develop. It always does sooner or later when two or more human beings get together.

When the small business pro encourages a little competition between departments (a technique highly recommended), he also increases potential friction.

To overcome friction, consider the organization chart technique. At a regular meeting with your key people say, "I think it is time we took a look at our organization on paper." Get a drawing pad (better still, a blackboard) and start sketching your organization chart.

Do this in front of the group, not before they come in. As you put the various boxes on that chart, ask the person whose department is being sketched in if that looks right to him. Stop frequently to ask the group, "Does that look right to you fellows?" They are helping you make their own organization chart!

As you go along you talk about teamwork, not crossing over departmental lines, all pulling together, etcetera. They will accept this at that time.

If someone is called out for a phone call, stop. Wait until he returns, because it is doing it together in front of each other that makes this technique effective.

When it comes to the two who are not getting along, put them at opposite sides of the chart. Keep asking if you are getting it right. Someone will speak up, "Well, it's all right as far as you've gone." Or something like that. Whoever says that, whoever enters a reservation, you can be fairly sure he is the one with whom you are going to have trouble. Often it is one of the men involved in the friction. The chip on his shoulder is beginning to show.

Avoid covering the hot spot till last. Purposely leave a man or department out, and apologize. Perhaps make it one of the contending departments to further goad those involved in the friction. Your purpose is to get the trouble out on the table, so give a few veiled jabs—but keep them veiled so they are assured you are impartial, even unaware of the friction. When the chart is finished, excuse yourself to visit the men's room. As you leave say, "Are you sure this is the way it is?" Your absence provides them a little more relaxed discussion.

When you come back, ask again or say, "Where were we?" Usually, by this time, someone will tell you that such and such is not being done the way it is on the chart. If the production and sales managers are arguing over shipping, for instance, maybe the production man will say that sales has been going directly to the shipping clerk and giving him orders, whereas the chart shows the shipping clerk works under production. Now you are getting somewhere.

Ask the production man, "You wouldn't want sales to go clear around through your department with every order, would you?" Draw this roundabout procedure on the chart with your finger. This puts production in the position of admitting it is his authority that is bruised rather than an organizational deficiency. Usually he will capitulate— especially if you give sales a stern admonition about not issuing direct orders to personnel in shipping but simply scheduling customers' requirements.

Perhaps it will not be that easy. You may have to suggest that since the two cannot seem to agree, possibly shipping ought to be moved into the sales department. The threat of losing part of his authority usually will bring the production man around to deciding he can get along with the sales department after all.

Because it plots the interworkings of the organization clearly in view of all, and draws the management team members into helping fill in the sketch, the organizational chart method quickly resolves friction in an unexplosive way. It also impresses the team with your leadership. You are doing the managing but in a way they can accept.

In closing the meeting, be sure to point out that this is a growing company so the chart as drawn is fine for today ... but may change next month. Then, tear it up or erase it. This makes the point that you are willing to accept change. That the men had better stay on their toes, as their jobs are not fixtures. And that they must also be ready to accept change from time to time.

Static organization charts stuck on the wall somewhere create more trouble than they solve. Follow through by having no organization chart in existence, only the ones drawn—and then erased—at these periodic meetings.

What not to do: Draw up a lovely chart. Have the draftsman do it up beautifully, maybe even in color, then distribute it to the interested parties. The management team did not participate in its creation. It is a fixed state of affairs with no encouragement or recognition of flexibility. It implies that when there is a change you will let them know by sending a new chart.

It is easy to see how well each chart is accepted by individual department heads. You can tell by the one which is pinned on his wall—and the ones conspicuously omitted.

That sets the company politicians to work buttering up the boss to get a slight improvement in their position on the chart. New employees are upset because maybe they did not understand it quite that way when they joined the company. Ten-year men are irritated because they see new men on their level. While the fixed organizational chart on the wall may provide status for one, it can be a "festering boil" on the neck of another.

Your company's human assets are not all on the payroll. Your lawyer, accountant, and other consultants can be similar assets (even if they sometimes seem like liabilities) if you know how to manage them. Internal selling techniques help.

This is especially true of getting your lawyer and accountant to work together.

All communication with your management team cannot be in meetings. The old personal touch must be practiced with individual managers. Do not take all your employees into your confidence all the time, even your entire management team. For instance, call the accountant only on financial matters and the production manager only on manufacturing affairs. It is just sensible use of time and avoids management by committee. Go to his office rather than ask him to come to yours; he will be more at ease while you ask your question.

The human mind is very complicated. There will be employees who will try to break through your best management psychology and do some internal selling on you. Like the guy who comes to see the boss and asks him some questions—but not the one he is aiming at. Maybe he will·ask if he can move his desk. You go over the situation with him, and since it is a minor matter but one which seems to be important to him, you grow expansive and say yes. Your guard is down as he takes a minute to pass the time of day.

"Oh, by the way," he interjects, "I was wondering . . ."

Here it comes! "By the way" is the most dangerous phrase in employees' vocabulary. Like the whistle before a bomb hits. He makes a big deal of moving his desk but only drops the real subject on you casually—and it probably has to do with a raise.

Well, that is internal selling.

If you cannot manage people, your business may simmer along on the rear burner, but some of the good employees you may have acquired will boil off and go elsewhere.

Given this choice—which places the small business pro squarely at the crossroads—most of us will choose the easier, more profitable, more fun path of agreeing to work with someone who can provide the management skills *we lack*.

All is not solved by making this decision, however. You must find the right man. If that is no problem, learning to work together may be.

That is the time to learn the value of incompatibility.

It is not necessary to be palsy-walsy with business partners or associates. It is not even desirable. "Business and pleasure don't mix" is an old adage that seems to be true. All that is necessary is to be able to get along together as adults. As long as you and your fellow owner, or management team members, are united behind common goals and are mature men and women who exhibit common courtesy and respect for the ideas of others, you can succeed famously without sharing your social lives.

A major bugaboo in big or small business is the belief that social life has to be built around business. Many of the fights and disrupting factors that break up companies get started at the social level. So-and-so's wife may displease one of the owners by something she says at the church social. What has that got to do with the owner's ability to work with Mr. So-and-so during business hours?

These things are so obvious. Yet every day we hear of problems caused by inability of small businessmen to separate their business lives from their social hours.

Since you need not be bosom friends to be partners, it follows that you can have little or nothing in common— except the business and its objectives. Personalities can be very different.

This may lead to incompatibility. You are an optimist, outgoing, people-oriented. Your partner is shy, soft-spoken, a doubter. So what? Those are the very traits which made you manager and him the financial man. (Think what would happen if he were sales manager and you the accountant!) Why shouldn't you be able to work together despite the fact you are naturally "incompatible" and would not choose each other for companionship under other circumstances?

Do not be afraid to hire department heads who are

completely opposite from you in personality. The lack of compatibility can be to the company's profit. Among other advantages, you will not be tempted to mix business with pleasure, or to waste time in irrelevant conversation.

Complementary executives in a company perhaps should be argumentative—and you, as the pro, know how to keep them sparking each other but not actually fighting. A mark of the sophisticated manager is his ability to integrate different viewpoints and personalities.

We are inclined to spend less time on things we dislike doing. Be objective about it, and hire people who are good at what you dislike. That frees you to concentrate on what you enjoy doing—which is what you do best.

Vice versa, you can afford to hire people who are weak in areas in which you are strong. The company is already covered there by your ability. Job descriptions help you select people for their rightness for the job rather than their compatibility with you.

Let your subordinates make mistakes!

Stand back and let your employees make little mistakes occasionally. Show them what they did and what they should have done instead. This most important technique helps them develop into more valuable team members. Someone said that "only a fool makes the same mistake twice." You may have some "fools" working for you but you will not know it unless you let them prove it.

Know your people intimately enough so that you can step in quickly and help them avoid making big, costly mistakes. You can afford to have a few little mistakes because it will help build your organization, but one big error can put you out of business.

When you see one of your guys about to make a fatal

mistake, step in fast; he will appreciate it too. You might say, "You know, Bill, I tried that once myself and it didn't work." If you handle it carefully, Bill will have more confidence in you and not be afraid to attempt changes in the future. Let your subordinates make little mistakes but not big ones.

Don't tell a good department head what to do. Instead, ask him what he plans to do. If he chooses a path different from yours, listen patiently to his reasoning. Is it sound and well-supported although different from what you would do?

Let him try it. If occasionally his reasoning is not sound, ask him leading questions. A good man will realize his error and will not need you to correct him. You must help him get to know you and your business objectives and why you think the way you do. This will enable him to gear his presentation to you so you both will have a better understanding.

A small manufacturing firm was purchased from the scientist who founded it. The founder had not spent much time there for several years. All decisions had been made jointly by five department heads who comprised the executive committee. The company was doing $300,000 in sales and losing $50,000 annually. The new owner's problem was to find out who had been making the wrong decisions that led to this condition.

Because all major decisions were joint it took a few months to discover a major incompetent. When he was discharged the other four loudly chorused that everything had been that *one* person's fault. When another man was let go, the remaining three said that all the problems were caused entirely by the two who had left.

This farce continued until finally all five were let go.

Only then could the new owner begin to make some sense of the place. The management team he inherited consisted of five incompetent "managers" who were all very nice people. They were wonderfully compatible with each other. The founder thought their compatibility indicated a good management team.

It is good psychology for everyone in management to feel involved in the whole company as long as you inspire them to do so intelligently.

For instance, a department head took a trip or a vacation. As soon as he left, people in his department started coming to you. Undoubtedly these people held back problems and questions until their boss had left.

They wanted to show their boss's boss they were capable.

Small businessmen have to be on to all these little tricks. It is nothing bad. In fact, it would be worrisome if the employees did not have the drive and ambition to want to call themselves to your attention.

When the department head returned, his staff told him there had been several problems which they had taken up with the big boss. Thus, they covered themselves and made it appear they were right on their toes too.

When the department head saw you he said, "Understand there were lots of problems the minute I left." So he felt important. The boss replied, "Yes, I guess so, but fortunately we were able to handle 'em all right."

Occasionally an executive will purposely leave just as a problem arises so the owner will realize how important the executive's job is. An unprofessional owner might pound the desk saying, "Why'd he go off without solving this thing!" Then he would immediately start calling him on the phone. Wrong!

When any team member is away, you *ought* to keep an eye on his department. You ought to go in, throw your feet on the desk, and ask, "Is there anything I can help you with?" This gives you an opportunity to listen to what has been going on. It is surprising what you will learn.

A professional small businessman plans his work and works his plan.

Charles D. Bond of Dynamics Research Corporation, a small business in a field dominated by space-age giants, says a good manager is "the man with a portable couch."

When you started out to be a small businessman, did you expect to end up a psychiatrist?

Labor Unions

Most businessmen, large or small, have, for generations, been fearful of unions and the detrimental effect on their business.

There have been all kinds of unions in our history, and some have been pretty bad. Perhaps some still are, or at least some of the leaders are.

However, there is no question that unions have done some good. Not so much good for the businessman but a great deal for the workers. If you have to face a union situation, here are a couple of ideas that might help.

Most union leaders today are well-educated, intelligent people. They are dedicated to their cause. The old ruffian, gangster, hoodlum type is the exception now. In dealing with union leaders, great care must be taken to treat them with respect. Do not look down on these people. We may not agree with them but we have to live with them.

When a union representative calls on you, treat him with dignity. Show him your place of business, introduce him to some of your employees, and invite him for lunch. I am not suggesting any phony approach. You should be sincere and treat him as well as you might treat an important customer. Communicating with him *is* most important. Try to understand him and his objectives, and help him see your side. At lunch have a drink or two.

If union men start passing out literature on the street in front of your business, invite them into your lobby, where it is warm. You will not gain anything by trying to make *their* job more difficult. You have nothing to hide and you should act so. Your employees will have more respect for you.

Treat the union organizer as well as the other unpopular guy who may pay you a visit some day, an IRS man. The IRS man probably will not let you pay for a drink, or lunch (he is not about to buy yours either). But a first-name relationship makes future negotiations easier.

You may want legal advice if the union shows up but *do not let your lawyer be present during negotiations.* Lawyers hired to fight the union indicate weakness of top management. The union organizer will be much easier to deal with if you keep your lawyer out of it. The union bargainer appreciates dealing with the head of the firm . . . and *you* can usually make a better deal.

The humble attitude is best. "I have had no experience with unions," you say, for example. "Please tell me how you operate," or "What would you do if your were in my position?" are good approaches. If you get pinned down, ask him if you could take it up with one of your *directors* —but do not mention your lawyer.

If you bring your lawyer into the fray they will bring in theirs. Your lawyer doesn't have the ability or experience to negotiate with their highly specialized labor lawyers.

They will beat yours every time. Be humble and let the union fellow help you. It is called ego. Get what you want by making him look good.

If your business does become unionized, all is not lost. You should maintain good rapport with the local union head. An occasional lunch or dinner will help. Treat him as if you understand why he is there (even if you don't). Actually, he can help you run your business.

Most small businessmen are spread too thin. We have to be everything to everyone in our businesses. If you are unionized, make the most of it.

The union can really assist you if you will let them. How? For one thing, they will help you with internal management problems. You no longer have to worry about "good old Jones" who has been with you so long. The company has outgrown him and you are probably paying him more than he is worth now. Should he have a raise? You cannot afford it, but now you can tell him to take it up with the union steward.

If the majority of your employees voted for a union, perhaps it is your fault anyway. Regardless, they are there. Face it! They can help raise production; they can help weed out nonproductive workers; keep the place clean; keep it more efficient; and help you make money. All this, if you will let them. Take them into your business confidence. When your sales are down, tell them. And when they go up, do likewise. Make them feel a part of your organization. They are anyway.

Like insurance, the union is important even though you may not like it. If they want to run that portion of your business, let them. Don't fight 'em, join 'em.

This should enable you to spend more of your valuable time in sales or developing new products. Or, better still, starting other new businesses.

CHAPTER XII

The No-Account
Executives

It is doubtful there is any business not concerned in one way or another with advertising.

Yet, common errors in advertising are the rule among too many small businessmen. Mostly they don't do any. Those who do, advertise grudgingly, as a "necessary evil." They are too tight to spend adequately for the advertising they do, so they get what they pay for—ads which represent them poorly. For the most part, they advertise merely to see their names in print, which is a fairly expensive ego trip.

There has been much use of the word "image" in recent years, which most small businessmen take to mean their own name. What it really means is the face your business presents to the public; how your customers and potential customers feel about your company. You have an image, whether you like it or not.

But is it a good one? Accurate? If everyone in town hates going to a certain gas station because the proprietor and his employees are rude and not helpful, it soon gets a poor image. Reputation is a better way of phrasing it. But it is an honest one, which the station deserves.

Is your company's reputation good? Does it deserve to be?

You can't fool people long. All the advertising in the world, telling what a fine place that gas station was, would not alter its image. People know better from personal experience.

This implies that every business, large or small, must have a good reputation.

First, it must have policies for doing business which merit a good reputation.

Secondly, it must get these policies across to the public in word and deed. The "word" part means advertising.

There is no excuse for bad public relations regardless of the size of your business. If your switchboard operator is snippy to callers, she can kill more sales than a good, hardworking sales rep can generate. Get rid of her.

If your product literature is poorly written, and insults the readers with poor grammar or unsupported claims, this is bad public relations just as surely as a rude employee. Get rid of it. Do it over.

If you are not qualified to do it yourself, get help.

Word-of-mouth is the best advertising. It is an implied endorsement every time. But you cannot count on getting it, and have no way of knowing when you do. Nonetheless, it is the ultimate desire of any public relations program.

By Any Name Would Smell

Advertising copywriters have been especially fond of Shakespeare's "a rose by any other name would smell as sweet."

Advertising. Promotion. Publicity. Merchandising. Marketing. Sales promotion. Public relations. Institutional. Direct mail. Media. Point of purchase. Image.

What do they mean? How do they differ? Which of them are useful to small business?

Many of the terms are interchangeable. All of them can be grouped under the heading "public relations," because all are concerned with effecting good business relations with the public, your customer.

Marketing refers to the planning, research, and statistics on which company sales projections and goals are based.

Merchandising is the promotional effort made for a product or service at the retail level, and especially at the point of purchase. Window displays, store banners, shelf stickers, even the label or packaging of the product are included. So are product demonstrations, giving samples, bill stuffers, special price offers.

Sales promotion refers to the effort made to assist salesmen selling the trade. It can include advertising and publicity, usually carried in trade publications, and a direct mail campaign to buyers or purchasing agents, as well as the material carried by the salesmen in the sales kit, such as catalog sheets, brochures and flyers, product demonstration materials, filmstrips, or movies.

Publicity refers to placing news and feature articles about a company or its products. Sometimes public relations is confused with publicity. Publicity is only one of many public relations tools.

Community relations, press relations, stockholder relations, employee relations, and other terms involving that oddball word "relations" describe a project or program aimed at the group mentioned in the first half of the phrase.

This does not exhaust the fancy terminology Madison Avenue has dreamed up to describe its services. This sampling ought to give you an idea of two problems, however.

First, that the ad men know how to make their jobs mystical and seemingly more important by surrounding them with confusing jargon.

Secondly, that most of the specialists who perform these functions are not needed by the majority of small businesses. Every business needs their *results*, however.

Big business can hire specialists for these jobs. The professional small business practitioner must learn to do them himself. That is a tall order, but in today's competitive situation they are among the most important business tools.

You don't *have* to learn them . . . if you can be sure your competitors won't either. On the other hand, if you become proficient at public relations planning, and learn how to do some of the technical jobs yourself, it may give you a powerful advantage over your competition.

The key to successful public relations is integration. This refers to smooth planning in which every promotional activity integrates, or meshes, with every other. For instance, if you are pushing a certain item in your ads, reinforce it by devoting window displays, points of purchase, direct mail, or publicity to the same item. Psychological studies reveal that people need several reminders before they act. Mrs. Dough may be intrigued by your ad for one-hour dry cleaning. When she is on her way to have something cleaned and sees the banner in front of your store, "Try Our One-Hour Service," this reinforcement of her original interest will bring her in the front door. They have to come through your door to get to your cash register. *Integrate* your promotion to notify passersby *this* is the place they saw advertised.

Or, if you are running four trade publication ads during the year, instead of having them all appear within the first two months, spread them out so that one appears each quarter. This keeps your name consistently in front of your customers.

If you are a small manufacturer, you can prepare such unique advertising that you will stand out despite the competition. You know your product best!

Of course, you have got the business to run, with sales, finance, production, shipping, the office, and other departments to worry about. And advertising is an art, though there is a science to it as well. Maybe you could use the assistance of specialists.

Professional, creative advertising agencies and other promotion and public relations consultants can do a great deal for a small business—provided they are guided and *forced to earn their keep*.

Advertising is not a necessary evil but a great opportunity open to all regardless of size. Really good professional counsel can help you grasp the opportunity.

Cases of this abound. Look at just one: Gallo Wine is not a small company, but the sales for its wine coolers were tiny when compared with the sales of beer companies like Budweiser and Miller and with those of the largest liquor companies. But through the imaginative, humorous, folksy ads for Bartles & James wine coolers, Gallo captured hundreds of millions of dollars of business taken away from companies with much larger ad budgets.

To start, choose an agency in which you will be one of the largest accounts. No matter how small your business there are agencies in your category.

Help each other grow. As you get better, you will increase your advertising budget and the agency will get bigger. Each needs the other; each has a stake in helping the other progress.

Be careful your agency does not outgrow you, or vice versa. For your company to grow takes considerable time, capital, equipment, new products, increased personnel, etcetera. For the ad agency to grow takes only a few more account executives.

Beware. Since it is easy for the agency to grow *faster* than your business, you may suddenly find yourself not getting the attention you need. You are now one of their smaller accounts. When this happens, start looking for a new agency.

Ad agency account executives, handling small business clients, seldom deserve the title. They are not executives at all. In a properly run agency they are *errand boys* who take your information and instructions back to the creative copywriters and designers who produce the advertising. Often their only executive ability is to have the latest Madison Avenue neckties, the proper shirts, the knowledge of how to drink martinis and pick up the check, and how not to step on the client's toes.

He is called an executive, but could he be one in your company? Your production manager, for instance? Fiscal executive? Department manager? More directly, could he be your sales manager? If not, don't hire him as your account executive—because sales help is what you want from your agency.

In hiring an agency, look beyond the account executive. Meet the agency owner. He is often a figurehead who bangs together the heads of his no-account executives. He dazzles them with his American Express platinum card and tells them who to call on next. And usually what to say.

You have to check him out because he sets the tone for his agency. But the really important people are the ones who produce the agency's product, its advertising. No-account executives seldom double in brass at this. Neither do owners. Copyrighting, designing, and the other technical functions which combine to produce advertising are specialties requiring natural ability, training, and experience.

There are two things you ought to know about these people in any agency you consider hiring. First, are they good? Second, are they given the freedom to produce the ads they are capable of—or do the no-account execs and the owner force them to produce what *they* think you want?

You hire an agency for its creative talent, not its management. You are a professional manager yourself, so why do you need agency "executives" standing between you and the talent? You don't. Except as errand boys and to keep the agency running smoothly so the creative talent can concentrate on producing fine ads for you.

Testing the Effectiveness of Your Ads

An old advertising story states that doctors' mistakes are buried, lawyers' are in jail, preachers' are in hell—but the ad man's mistakes are in four-color two-page spreads in *Time* magazine. The moral is that you cannot always predict response to advertising.

To overcome this, big advertisers and agencies employ copy testing. An interviewer stands in Grand Central Terminal or on Main Street asking passersby to choose between copy themes, illustrations, or complete ads. This has serious limitations, but for small business it does not matter. *You cannot afford it anyway.*

How can you test your advertising, in whatever medium, both before and after it appears?

First, adopt simple rules of good taste, carefully applied to your product or situation. Don't try to be funny. Don't try to be cute. Please don't be corny. Naturally, don't be vulgar. And don't brag all the time. Your ads are printed representations of yourself. Make them reflect your good manners and good taste.

Rising sales are only one indication of ad effectiveness. Some small companies grow in spite of poor or nonexistent advertising. This does not indicate that advertising has no effect, however. If sales grew 4% without ads, or with mediocre ads, the increase might have been 14% or 24% with a good advertising program. Really fine advertising has made many companies, many products.

Advertising is big business. But much of it is ineffective, wasteful, and wide of the mark. Big business may feel it can afford such luxuries. Rare is the small business that can, or should. If dollars are going to be wasted, there are better ways to do it than by purchasing bad advertising. More enjoyable, too.

CHAPTER XIII

Moonlight Sonata and Other Music

HARNESSING the services of outside professionals will set you on the right course. Organizing a management team will make your company more productive. Selling a smaller market, which you can dominate, will enable you to compete. But profits may still elude you.

Profits come to small business when all aspects of its operation are humming smoothly. There is little margin for error. Here are some operating hints which have proven effective for the profitable conduct of small business.

Moonlight Sonata

Research and development has become extremely important to small business.

One tremendous advantage of big business is its majority share of government-sponsored research. Most of the current technological advances are coming from R & D programs under contract with Department of Defense, NASA, and other Federal agencies. Although official public policy is to make any commercially applicable results available to all business simultaneously (once they are declassified and released), the company which performed the R & D has the lead by virtue of its experience.

It is very difficult for small business to obtain government research contracts, and the average small concern is usually unable to support its own internal research program. (See Chapter XVII.)

Yet it is becoming clear that research is essential to survival in many industries. Whether the need is for product research, market research, or whatever, small business, like all businesses, must do some.

The answer for your company may be in the army of moonlighters—persons who work more than one job.

A Labor Department study released not long ago showed that 5.7 million persons were moonlighting. They accounted for 5.0% of all employed workers, and the percentage has held near that figure for at least the last decade, and probably higher now.

The average moonlighter devotes 13 hours weekly to his second job. And professional, technical, and management workers are the most active categories of moonlighters.

What a boon to small business, which cannot afford the full-time salaries of these experts. By hiring a top mechanical or electrical engineer to help you develop your new product, you can get the best men in the field—at a fraction of normal cost.

Teachers are an excellent source of moonlighting. The reason is apparent: they need the extra money.

The use of moonlighters is not limited to research or development. Tax experts, advertising men, production engineers, retail specialists, chemists—nearly every phase of business has the possibility of utilizing moonlighters to get expert help at low cost.

A good ad agency might not be interested in your small company. But the same art director or copywriter who would be handling your account at the agency might be glad to work for you as a moonlighter.

Top engineers and others who may not be tempted by the money may agree to moonlight for a percentage, or for stock options in your company. As salaried employees, no capital gains opportunities are open to them in their regular jobs. The availability of capital gains appreciation over a period of years could have more appeal than cash.

On the subject of new product development—which is one of the most active moonlighting areas for small business—a good way to conduct a continuing R & D or market research program is to allocate a certain percentage of your sales to it, then use that money to hire the best moonlighters you can find. This puts it on a regular basis just like accounting and sales. The only difference is that the personnel involved are part-time. Pay the moonlighter on a contract basis, keeping him off the payroll if you can.

No Decision

Decisions, decisions, decisions. Not only do they account for most of a businessman's working day but his success depends on making the right ones at least most of the time.

Many of the decisions you make every day are unnecessary!

> *Next time you think you have to make a decision, ask yourself what harm would be done if you didn't make it. How much is it going to hurt the business if you don't decide now?*

If it can wait, put it off! You will be able to make a better decision at a later date because you will have time to acquire more facts on which to base it.

Though you may hire outside professionals to help in some areas, they are not always available when it is time to make decisions.

As a famous Englishman phrased it, "When in doubt do nothing." Sometimes the best decision to make is *not* to make one.

Big business follows this rule. Probably not purposely but because of red tape and the number of people on the corporate ladder that have to okay everything. The result is the same, ironically. Decisions are slow getting made, so by the time the problem reaches top management the right decision is more obvious.

If you have nothing to lose by not making a decision today, don't make it.

You will know more tomorrow and perhaps even more the next day.

Pensions and Profit Sharing

Two big business techniques which work for larger small businesses are profit sharing and pension trusts.

Consider these advantages: Profit sharing and pensions can help small business compete with big business for key men.

Contributions to profit sharing and pension plans are deductible.

If your company is in the 34% tax bracket—which only means it is making a profit of over $25,000—it costs only $.66 on the dollar.

It is better to pay some of this money to your key men than to IRS

Profit sharing and pensions give employees security and confidence in the company and its management. They can be a major factor in employee morale.

Along with helping your employees, you help yourself most of all. The owner gets the lion's share.

Assuming your company is a corporation, you are president or an officer, your salary is the highest in the company. Since profit sharing and pension trusts are usually based all, or part, on salary, you will be the big winner. Since any cash paid to you as profit sharing might qualify as regular income, you may have to pay normal tax on it. But pension fund contributions are deductible providing they meet certain IRS requirements.

Such combination profit sharing–pensions are called qualified plans. (They don't rule out a special pension trust for executives.) Some profit sharing is on a cash plan, where employees receive their share each year in cash. This soon becomes a Christmas bonus and is assured each year as part of the salary; not effective. This sacrifices the loyalty-building advantage of a qualified plan. An employee who has been with your company a few years and has a tidy sum built up in a pension fund or profit sharing plan is bound to be a harder worker and better booster for the company.

Payments from pension trusts and profit sharing are usually handled so they qualify for special tax rates later on.

You cannot become wealthy on a salary. These two devices can help you get more wealth from your company along with capital gains.

A pension trust ought to be looked into first. It is usually more effective if limited to a few key executives and very important employees.

When your pension plan is operating smoothly, and a

few years have passed to prove that funding it is no problem, look into profit sharing. This is a more effective management tool if all employees are included. Seniority and salary ought to be important parts of the formula, but incentives and rewards for especially fine performance need not be excluded.

The easiest way to do something about these is to call your life insurance agent. His company has highly paid specialists who will tailor-make plans for your situation. Of course, he will try to sell you more insurance while he is there, but so what? Perhaps you need more.

Your company must be making a profit. And hopefully is going to continue doing so.

At the beginning of 1967 there were an estimated 55,000 qualified profit sharing plans in effect, embracing over six million participants. These profit sharing funds have assets over $25 billion. Today these assets are a great deal more.

The idea of sharing in the profits of a cooperative effort are as old as organized human endeavor. Mediterranean fishermen shared in the catch in antiquity, just as New England whalers did in more recent years.

A famous early American fiscal expert, Albert Gallatin, Secretary of the Treasury under Presidents Jefferson and Madison, and one of our first industrialists, instituted the first American profit sharing plan in 1797.

Joseph B. Meier, long a leader of the Council of Profit Sharing Industries, says every employee lucky enough to work for a company with profit sharing is a capitalist. To support his position, he merely quotes Webster, who defines a capitalist as, "a person who owns or controls large amounts of accumulated wealth used in business." Profit sharing funds are invested in business, often in the company whose employees they cover.

This highlights the major benefit of profit sharing. By giving employees a stake in an investment, they are forced to think about the nature of business, of capital, and of employees' relationships with management and the company. Employees who have considered such business problems are bound to have more understanding of management and be more willing to work harder to help the company succeed—and profit.

How else could you get your employees to sympathetically understand the facts of business, and their place—and yours—in it?

Perhaps it is your social responsibility to consider it.

Cash Position and the IRS

If your company ever gets a lot of cash in the bank you are in trouble. Double trouble.

First, management may not be doing its job. Because that job is to keep the capital working. Cash in the bank may be all right for widows, but not for a small businessman.

Worse, the Internal Revenue Service is going to keep an eye on you. When any company has lots of cash floating around, IRS expects it to start paying dividends.

As a small business pro, your company is doing really well. Your salary is comfortable. Enough profits have been earned over the years to start Businesses 2, 3, and 4. Profit sharing and pension plans are keeping key men and other employees happy—and pouring additional funds into your estate and theirs.

You really do not want to declare any dividends because they are subject to double taxation. First, the corporation tax and then again on the stockholders personally. Yet, you have all this loose cash lying around.

What can you do?

First, you can make sure the company has some outstanding bank loans which you may need in case business falls off. Since your company owes substantial debts, it obviously cannot pay dividends.

Or, you can claim it is a fund laid aside for the next year or two, when you have reason to believe business will not be so good due to heavy competition or some other reason you know is just over the horizon.

You can always be going to expand. But *have your plans in your file* outlining the expansion. Have something on paper, not just a vague idea in your head.

Similarly, you can claim large amounts are being set aside for a new product development program. Again, keep such a program outline handy, complete with reports from your marketing and production people and perhaps some ideas from your ad agency and lawyer. Have it on paper.

These are legitimate reasons for a small business to build up large cash reserves.

If IRS gets you into a position where discussions on such subjects are necessary, it is wise to build a good relationship with the tax men. Cultivate an informal relationship with them. Don't be phony. Be yourself. Take time to get to know these people as humans. You are bound to have some things in common and may, hopefully, find a real friend, although I doubt it. IRS investigators appear to be rewarded on some kind of commission basis (which I do not understand).

One other thing IRS watches carefully is companies with the same ownership which do business with one another. If your store leases space from your real estate concern, red lights flash on in your tax agent's brain. Be sure you and your accountant work out the patterns by which your companies buy and sell to one another. Usually it is wise to have the prices charged as fair. Be very reasonable, as if they were separate companies. Extra low or extra high prices will usually attract IRS attention unless they can be justified.

Patents and Ethics Don't Mix

At present most U.S. patents are not worth much, especially in electronics and other advanced technology. They may impress your friends and board of directors, but as practical, money-making business tools they are nearly worthless.

Current practice is to go ahead and use any patent when needed, regardless of ownership. Though this is clearly stealing it is also practical. The product making use of someone else's patent(s) will be either successful or it won't. If it isn't you would have increased your losses by paying royalties. And the patent owner has nothing to sue for if the product flops.

If the product succeeds you will undoubtedly get a registered letter from some inventor's lawyer, which you should ignore. Next comes a visit from a lawyer, which you can't ignore. He will very gently accuse you of several things but will handle it in a friendly fashion because what he wants from you is a flow of money to his client (and him) from continued success of your product using his client's patent.

After a year of negotiation one of two things will occur:

The patent in question will now be obsolete, so you won't need it any longer. Thus, there's nothing to pay royalties for. The lawyer will try to recoup something from his efforts by slapping you with a suit for the period in which you did "borrow" the patent, but it is easily settled out of court, as a rule, and usually for not too much money. Even if it costs a lot you should have made plenty on the use of the patent.

Or, you can make a better deal then, better than you could have had at first by going to the patent owner before you went into production. One reason is that the patent owner is aware your product has been developed to a point where you can more easily circumvent the patent.

Also, the patent now has *less* time to run. Perhaps you have made some improvements in the patent, or found some weaknesses, which strengthen your bargaining position.

If your company desires to use a patent held by one of the big corporation patent pools, go ahead and use it. If you have been successful and they seek you out, you may have to pay royalties. However, before you do, be sure to get a written answer to this question. You should ask them if they have a plan to continue to protect the patent from all other unauthorized users. It certainly is ridiculous for your company to pay a royalty if there are other rascal companies who are not. This puts the large corporation patent holder in the position of having to constantly police the whole field. This is costly and does not enhance their public image. Frequently they will not bother.

Even the Supreme Court does not protect the little patent holder today. Patent litigation is very costly for both sides. It requires many experts for testimony and in general benefits only the lawyers. Therefore, patent owners are usually anxious to make a deal rather than sue.

Big business frequently uses any patent it needs. If the

corporation's patent department feels the patent is a reasonably strong one, from which litigation may result, a contingency fund is set aside—much like a royalty but kept by the corporation.

If litigation comes, this amount is available to pay costs of the suit and then to make a settlement or, better, agree to pay on future sales. Because patent cases drag on and on a settlement is almost always the best way out for the little patent owner. Even sizable companies whose patents are infringed upon would rather get something via settlement than be bothered with a long court case.

If litigation does not occur, the contingency fund is added to the profit later on.

Small business is forced to adopt this patent policy because big business, with all its other advantages, is following it. If a small business practitioner does not do this, he is giving his big business competitors another advantage.

Small concerns can borrow, most easily, patents held by big ones. Big business will generally hesitate at entering a suit against a little guy over patent infringement, since it hurts its public image, and may possibly cause the anti-trust department of the Federal Trade Commission to look into the matter.

When a small businessman I know bought a company a few years back, it was paying royalties on five patents under contracts. Four were held by giant companies and one was owned by an independent inventor. The company paid, even though it was losing $40,000 a year.

The new owner immediately stopped all payments. Five registered letters came and were duly ignored. Then five black briefcases came to call, one by one.

"Why are you violating my client's royalty agreement?"

But the new owner had a ready answer. "I am so busy

trying to stop losing money here that I can't be bothered with the royalty."

In effect, he laughed in their faces.

"But why did you stop now after the company paid so regularly all these years?"

"Here's why," said the new owner, and showed them the company's financial statements.

He never heard again from any of them.

Which is understandable. The name of the royalty game is money. If he was not making any they could not get any. So they could not be bothered wasting any more time on him.

"One-Way" Communications

The traditional way businessmen communicate is by letter. But built into their system and thinking are secretaries, office staff, typewriters, letterheads, dictating machines, and the other expensive and necessary paraphernalia for writing, receiving, and filing business letters.

. Letters are *one-way* communications. They state your side of the story but give you no way of telling how it is received.

A letter commits you, on paper, to whatever you write. Not just legally but in every way. If you ask an embarrassing question in a letter, you have no way of knowing, or doing, anything about it. Very few people will write back and tell you. Because it is embarrassing they want to forget it as fast as they can.

If you do not know what a potential customer is thinking, mentioning quantity or price in a letter, on paper, can cause him to lose interest. Or enter a smaller order than he would have placed had he been sounded out more carefully.

Alexander Graham Bell gave us the tool to avoid these problems.

On the phone you can feel your way. You can inject your personality through voice inflection which also conveys emphasis.

More important, by listening carefully you can tell how your message, or proposal, is being received. Phoning is *two-way* communication.

If you meet resistance or see that your proposal is running counter to the ideas of the person on the other end of the line, you can alter your approach on the instant. If the person you are calling does not understand, you can educate him right then.

With the court-enforced breakup of AT&T and the resulting fierce competition for long distance business, rates have been plummetting. At the same time, the cost of an average business letter—secretarial time, cost of paper, envelope and stamp, machinery required to type, copy, your time to dictate—has soared to over $20.00. There are not many places you can't call for an hour for under $20.00. Thus, using the phone for business communications is almost always cheaper and better than writing.

Letters have their place. Occasionally the subject is so complicated it must be put on paper so it can be studied. Formal quotations ought to be on paper. Unfortunately, small business cannot get rid of all the office overhead completely.

But most of us have much more of it than we need. Several companies, according to telephone company propaganda (which sounds logical), even found they had too many salesmen. The majority of a salesman's time is spent in travel between calls and waiting to see people. Telephone selling helps.

Among the success stories Ma Bell likes to recite are:

Oregon Marine Supply Company which increased profits by 20.5% when it introduced a planned telephone selling program. Commercial Office Supply Company, Philadelphia, which says it not only increased sales but improved customer service—very important in the office supply business where many lines are handled and often sold in small quantities. Lakeside Manufacturing, Inc., Milwaukee, which has 2,200 dealers for its product line, has no (zero) salesmen in the field because it uses strictly telephone sales on a *nationwide basis*. The company president says the system cut the cost of an average sales call from $30 to $1.50!

There must be something to it. Chances are that many of the advantages of face-to-face selling are retained by phoning without the time wasted in waiting rooms and front seats of automobiles.

All these companies are in the small business category. Needless to say, if you need further evidence of the value of the phone to your business, the telephone company will be happy to supply it.

What's more important is that your customer may prefer it. Bell's literature quotes one manufacturer: "Some of our older accounts preferred doing business by phone. It cuts down on that long parade of salesmen and it provides instant response."

On the subject of telephoning, one public relations area overlooked by too many businesses is telephone etiquette. One that bothers me personally is to get a call, have the switchboard or your secretary say so-and-so is calling, then pick up the phone and find that Mr. So-and-so is not on the line yet himself.

Be on the line when the person you are calling picks up the phone.

Another hint is *not* to have your operator, or secretary, ask who is calling. If your line is busy, OK, but if not let the call go right through to you.

One small manufacturer doing business nationally with approximately 100 customers installed a second phone on his desk with a private and unlisted number. The president then wrote all his customers a personal letter stating that if you have a complaint or problem or want to place an order, call me personally, *collect*. He also stated that "no one else would ever answer this phone." His personal touch increased sales and provided the president with a direct contact with the field. It was so successful that his competitor did the same, later on.

PART FOUR

CONSTRUCTIVE THINKING

CHAPTER XIV

The Victorious Attitude

SBA's management research reports indicate the average small businessman generally rejects outside help. A look at most of the published material offered him suggests one reason. It is written *about* small business, not *for* it. Most of it lacks color and is written by professorial types having little actual small business experience.

Here are a few operating tips and tactics collected by a small businessman from experience in his own businesses and his observation of others. Some of these suggestions may work for you.

Psychology and Small Business

Despite the success of the play and movie *How to Succeed in Business Without Really Trying*, it is not so. You may be lucky. Business success may almost reach out and grab you. But you must really try.

In fact, you will work your head off. There is a way to make it easier. That way begins with the proper attitude. I call it the victorious attitude, the state of mind that assumes from the beginning, in all you do, that you are going to come out on top.

When you approach a customer, your lawyer, or your

banker, have a victorious attitude. Be assured you are going to get the order or the loan or the help you need. Chances are you will, because *confidence is catching.*

Negotiating agreements with your customers, suppliers, associates, banker, and others is often a battle of wits. The person who demonstrates by his attitude that he will not be defeated raises doubts in his adversaries. You know from your own experience that self-doubt is a destroyer. You cannot win if you doubt you can.

Doubt is natural to everyone, since we all have our limitations. Wiping doubt from your mind is a technique which can be learned. The logic of it goes like this:

There are limits to what Man can do. He cannot fly or see through walls. But neither can he do anything about these limitations. Therefore, why worry about them—or let them deter you? Instead, spend your effort succeeding in spite of them by finding out how to get around them. Instead of thinking of reasons why you cannot do a certain thing, think of ways to accomplish it with the tools at hand.

Accept what you cannot change; change what you are capable of; and if you cannot distinguish the one from the other, hire someone who can.

Why worry about something you cannot control or even influence? That is unprofessional.

You are adding an unnecessary burden. Psychologists have theories about why people worry even when they know it is useless to do so. Some worry is actually mental illness.

Most business worry is simpler than that. If you face a hard day's work, don't worry about it. It is easier to tackle the work than to worry about it.

The best answer for a worrier is to force yourself to

start working on some important job. It may be difficult, but once you are involved in it you become so absorbed that the worry is lost in the shuffle. It may reappear, in which case you have to push yourself into tackling another job.

One technique that works on worry, or looking-out-the-window fever, is to quickly call and make an appointment with someone. Your lawyer, maybe, or a customer. Since most businessmen are socially oriented, you will get your mind away from your worry and might learn something valuable. The pressure of the relationship with another person is a handy crutch to get rid of worry and get you going again.

Psychology is a big subject, but a few simple tricks and techniques may help. They are worth a try.

When you are with a salesman or customer, or in an important negotiation of any kind, where do you normally sit? In any chair that happens to be available?

Wrong! Where you sit may have important bearing on your ability to horse-trade your way to a more profitable deal. Sit with your back to the light. This puts you in the shadow so your adversary cannot look into your eyes and face to discover what is going on inside your mind. He is in the light, however, so you can look closely at him.

Next time you are having a business lunch, watch the battle for the right chairs as other groups come in and take their tables. Or watch the sheep who lead themselves to slaughter by meekly taking the chair nearest them—or that is offered them by the guy they are negotiating with.

An attractive woman knows this technique well, except that she does the reverse. She grabs the chair which faces the light so her beauty will be radiated.

Bankers do it. They make you sit with the light shining

on you at the loan officer's desk. The banker even goes a step further in this applied psychology and makes you sit where you cannot get your feet under the desk as he can. So you cross and uncross your legs uncomfortably, right out in the open with nothing to hide behind—usually in an uncomfortable chair.

Standard police techniques have long operated on this principle. That is why they put a spotlight on a criminal when questioning him. You can get some benefit of this "third degree" by being careful to grab the right chair. Try it. See if it doesn't make a difference. Rearrange your own office accordingly.

Some put on their glasses as a further foil. A few businessmen who spend a lot of time negotiating have gotten glasses even though they do not need them, for this purpose. Should you be outmaneuvered in getting the seat with your back to the light, putting on your glasses may help.

In smaller communities, where most business is small, there sometimes exists subtle unfriendly sentiment among businessmen. Everyone is friendly to your face, but if you are a little more successful than they, the bunch is likely to run you down behind your back. Even your friends and associates are swept along in this negative psychology. It is usually subconscious and might be referred to as "subconscious jealousy."

It is human nature to compare. We all do it. When subconscious jealousy enters the comparison, it may become harmful. How many times have you heard someone say, "I understand John's company is in trouble." Compare that with the times you have heard, "I hear John's company is doing great." You will hear some of the latter, of course, but far more of the former.

Man develops his ego by comparing. Little people get a subconscious lift if their friend's business is having trouble and theirs is not. It is a subtle thing. The danger is that it makes us think we are doing well—not by building our own businesses but by tearing down the businesses we compare with ours.

It is easiest to fall into this about competitors. We build ourselves up by knocking them. Nothing really happens except in our own minds. It is merely a substitute for getting off the old duff and outperforming our competition.

Forget your competitor as a person. Don't think of him, think of his business. Think of that only as a statistic, a set of figures you must do better than; a game to win, an opposing team you must beat. If you cannot lick him in size or volume, beat him in quality or service.

What do you care about the personal life of your competitor? What has that got to do with business? That has nothing whatever to do with competing in business where you are out to win. So he is better-looking than you, can play golf or bridge better than you, sings in the church choir and gets elected to the Chamber of Commerce, or his wife is more beautiful than yours, and his kids are smarter and better athletes than yours. So what? The question is, is he winning the business competition over you?

It is cold comfort for him to be able to say that he can beat you on the golf course when you are beating him in bank deposits or capital gains.

As competitors, you and he have far more in common than in opposition. The products you sell compete because they are similar. Yours may be higher quality, but he has you beaten on price. Looked at in the light of modern marketing, maybe you two ought to be working together to assure a good overall market for both your products rather than fighting over whether they buy his brand or yours. You may beat each other's brains out and both go out of business.

Collusion

"Collusion" is defined by Webster as "a secret agreement or cooperating for a fraudulent or deceitful purpose." The writer is not recommending anything fraudulent or even deceitful. The word is used here primarily for emphasis and for lack of a better one. A LESSON LEARNED FROM BIG BUSINESS. The *Wall Street Journal* carried this item on its front page:

> AUTO ROW AMITY blooms in Sacramento, Calif., where old friend Bob Batey, a Chevrolet dealer, and Frank Cate, a Ford dealer, team up in a joint TV advertising campaign: While other dealers look askance, Mr. Batey says, "I think we're getting more results for one half the cost."

I wrote to Mr. Cate at once:

> Mr. Frank Cate
> 9499 Highway 99
> Elk Grove, California
> Dear Mr. Cate:
>   Presently I am writing a book for small business and I am specially concerned with the need for small businessmen to do some constructive rethinking of traditional methods. I was, therefore, very interested to see the *Wall Street Journal* article concerning your joint advertising campaign with Mr. Bob Batey.

As a small businessman myself, I think that we should consider more closely the advantages of cooperative strategy. The banks, the government, and big business certainly use cooperative practices for the sake of greater efficiency from their point of view. There seems no reason why small business should not learn from their experience.

I would very much appreciate it if you or Mr. Batey could outline the way in which you worked out your campaign and the factors which you feel underline its success. I would be grateful for any statistics or other information you could furnish me on the costs and results of your venture.

Very truly yours,

His reply was encouraging. The two competitive dealers, located side by side, are jointly on TV, in newspaper ads, in a local TV guide, and on billboards. Cate reported this joint venture "has proved both unique and most of all profitable." He also stated:

At present we are on TV in color . . . We have created a type of advertising there that has caused a lot of talk, and will continue to pay in good returns for some time. I would be most happy to have you publish our good neighbor policy, and how small businesses can prosper pulling together for their share of the *same market* and getting it.

This is a classic case where the common problems these two new-car dealers face outweigh competitive considerations. They are situated in a suburb miles from a large city with its many new-car dealers. Instead of giving up to the powerful competition of the big city, they are going out to get business there! They have erected a billboard at the freeway exit to lure customers from the city as they pass by.

It is doubtful either of them alone could have afforded color television commercials, outdoor advertising, etcetera. Their pooled budgets make it possible.

There is not a more competitive, rough-and-tumble business than new cars. If these dealers can cooperate for mutual advantage, it ought to give the rest of us some ideas.

We should cooperate through chambers of commerce and trade associations. This collectivism has not begun to develop.

Apply this same theory to your particular company. Get to know your competitor. Even if he is quite a bit larger, or smaller, you stand to gain by working together, jointly battling everyone else instead of each other.

Of course, don't gang up on a third competitor or anything like that. It may be against the law. Big companies *never* get together and squeeze out an unwanted or uncooperative competitor. They would not do such a thing . . . because it is illegal. Granted, supermarket prices appear to be fixed. And gas station prices are exactly the same. Government bids have the same price or only one that is lower. It is just happenstance.

If you decide to use some of the standard operating procedures of big business, just be careful not to get caught! If 6 million small businesses used these tactics, the government would have to have an "Anti-SBA" and there would be no room in the jails for the other criminals.

Labor unions are an example of individual workingmen cooperating instead of battling one another for raises, promotions, and benefits. Big labor has been accused of collusive tactics similar to those for which big business is often criticized. These tactics are very effective for big organizations. There are many things small business can profitably borrow from the big boys.

You are constantly battling collusion or collectivism and not just from big business and labor. Through the bar associations, lawyers belong to what has been described as "the world's most powerful labor union." Certainly it forges advantages for lawyers in every possible way, even if it has to pass—or kill—legislation to do it.

The way lawyers and bankers seem to be in constant touch is another example. Also, the way bankers check with one another on loan applicants. To overcome these practices and substitute for them competition between professionals, it makes sense to switch lawyers, bankers, accountants, and insurance agents fairly often.

The simplest way for small business to battle these practices is to fight fire with fire and adopt these same techniques in its own behalf.

Small business operators ought to work together—nothing fraudulent, of course. We have no strong national organizations as other professionals do. Perhaps we should have! Meanwhile, let's get together on a local level at least.

There are many other lessons to be learned from big business. Some are positive, showing how we can do things. Some are negative, teaching us to avoid others.

To initiate constructive rethinking of traditional methods, such as substituting cooperation for competition, it takes a confident small business pro. One who is not always worried about his business but who dares to try new methods to attain new profitability. In other words, one who has a victorious attitude.

Small business practitioners with victorious attitudes

are not afraid to borrow methods from big business. For instance, big business seldom holds a grudge. Individuals within a big company may, but the overall corporate policy seldom stoops to such foolishness.

A small manufacturer won a large judgment over one of the giants a few years ago. It was a long battle with teams of lawyers and experts on both sides. He won because he came up with angles on the case which convinced the jury.

Only a few days had elapsed since the judgment was awarded when he was called on by representatives of one division of the big company he had beaten in court. He did not know what was up and was apprehensive.

But big business became that way by realizing if you can't lick 'em, join 'em. To his amazement that is why these men were there. From the facts revealed about his company in the court case, and in their investigation, they realized he was a pro. Their visit was for the purpose of offering him regional representation—in another of his businesses—of one of their product lines.

They apparently figured anyone smart enough to beat their best brains was a man they wanted on their team.

It was a good deal so the small businessman welcomed it. The big company sent a credit man to examine his books as part of routine preparations for awarding the franchise. The day he arrived the check for the legal settlement came in the mail. The credit man began asking the usual questions. When he inquired what financial shape the company was in currently, the small businessman showed him his own company's check for a substantial sum. There were no more questions. His credit was quickly approved. Talk about having fun in business!

CHAPTER XV

How to Keep Score

ONE thing about falling in love with your business is that you may get too serious and spoil the fun.

Business is fun if you are a professional.

Fun and a game. You love matching wits, the competition, the many "opponents" you face. The thrill of challenge. The pleasure of succeeding. The trials of failing.

Business is fun but not enough small businessmen realize—or admit—they are having fun.

What is wrong is just the opposite because *not* having fun can make you overly serious. Then you smother your business. Kill it with love. Tense up, awkward as an overanxious lover.

Handling yourself so you enjoy business is part of professionalism because it keeps you loose, relaxed.

Having fun in business keeps your sense of humor. When you can laugh at yourself, your company, other businessmen and business itself, you retain your perspective and keep your objectivity. You don't tense up. Professional businessmen must be objective. As much as humanly possible, they have to be that way all the time. Like a surgeon performing delicate operations every day. Contemplate the results if he tenses up.

It is hard to enjoy your work when you are deathly

serious about it. This does not mean it is not important to you. It is so important that you should refuse to foul it up by losing your perspective and objectivity.

It is ironic, but the more fun you have the more successful you will be. The tighter and touchier you are, the more goofs you will make with subsequent detraction from your success.

Three arguments might be offered against having fun in your business.

1. "This is serious with me. I've got a wife and family to support and have to make money. It's not a game."
2. "Business with me is just a means to an end, a way to support my family and pay my bills. But it's not *really* important, I mean, not to the real problems of the world. I'd prefer to be doing something socially significant."
3. "It's big business's world today. I'm just a small businessman. I have to keep my nose right to the grindstone to stay alive."

When you don't have fun in business, money becomes an end in itself. Each dollar is watched as if it had a life of its own, almost like a son or daughter. Professional businessmen, with a carefully worked out plan, do not care about money per se. It is merely a way of *keeping score*, to know whether they are losing or winning the game. If it were not, men already wealthy would work for nothing or not work at all. They demand profit and income on their business deals even while they are giving away millions to philanthropy, in order to keep matching wits, keep competing, keep playing the game and having fun. Money is their way of keeping score.

The professional small businessman's overall personal plan permits him to look beyond the individual dollar and see his future. Without planning he could not see the capital gains for the cash register.

By having fun in business you can also make more money. Isn't this great! It is one of life's rare opportunities to have your cake and eat it. It is one reason the pro thinks business is the most fun in life.

Because having fun makes more profit, it also enables you to do more good. The bigger you build your business, the more people you hire, the more goods your business purchases . . . the more you are building your community. If everyone in the world had an opportunity for a good job at a decent income, it would solve many of our current problems. *You*, Mr. Small Business Man, can do great good right in your own business and have fun at it, making a profit. What is more socially significant than that?

If you really do not enjoy business, you probably should get out of it. That is not the problem with most of us. We never would have entered business if we did not like it. But many, maybe even most, small businessmen are afraid to *admit* they have fun in business.

You know the type. When he comes home from the "office" (whether it is a gas station or machine shop) he tells his wife and kids only what a hard day he had. How tired he is. As if there were something wrong with enjoying oneself. Especially at one's work.

A pro tells his family, in excited words, how he faced the competition on a deal and pulled it off. Or the suspense of trying to sell a new big customer. Of the stimulation he feels in designing a new product and the thrill when it goes into production and orders roll in.

In sports, when the professionals get together the talk

turns to sports. Pro businessmen do the same. Although they do not allow themselves to fall in love with a single company or industry, they love business.

When a pro baseball or football player is traded to another team he plays just as hard. He had not fallen in love with his former club.

To the man on the street, the small business professional life seems ideal. As soon as you do not work from nine to five daily, people think you are retired. Since the professional small business practitioner may not *have* to go to any of his places of business at any special time, each day he is accused of "goofing off" or being retired. But his life is better than retirement. He has the fun of his businesses yet free time whenever he wants it. And he earns far more than retirement income could ever provide.

The work he does, the problems he faces, illustrate the fun of business for a successful pro. Here is an actual list taken from the daybook of a small businessman who owns five companies:

PROBLEMS TO BE SOLVED NEXT QUARTER

1. Negotiate a new franchise contract.
2. Check morale in production department.
3. Close new product sales deal.
4. Open up Western territory.
5. Expedite and approve plants of new plant addition.
6. Invite Joe (sales manager) for dinner to discuss more sales for next 6 months.
7. Bring estate planning up to date with lawyer and accountant.

8. Find a Canadian small company for merger or affiliation.
9. Institute a profit sharing to augment pension plan?
10. Obtain a new product for Company No. 3.
11. Purchase more real estate for Company No. 4.
12. Lunch with Fred (bank president) to discuss financing plans for the next 6 months.

The excitement and fun of working out these problems is beyond comparison with slaving at a desk in someone else's business. The successful pro spends his time on policy decisions, not detail; planning and dreaming and scheming, not operations. He has a staff to handle operational details. They do the work. He has the fun. And he pockets the profits and builds more equity.

Objectivity is the most important quality in business professionalism. Having fun in business and treating money as the means of keeping score enable the small business operator to remain objective. They are the marks of a pro.

The unanswered question is how to become a pro. What techniques and abilities distinguish him? How does he approach and solve the problems all small businessmen grapple with?

There is no simple formula. The education of a small business professional is not taught in schools—even business schools. It can only be learned in the world's largest university, old Hard Knocks U.

Yet, if a small businessman will dedicate himself to professionalism, and if he avoids falling in love with a particular business, he may become wealthy.

By logically and energetically applying these principles to his business (businesses, rather), he can *hardly avoid* making a great deal of money, among other satisfactions and contributions to his community.

This does not mean he can merely pledge to do these things then sit back and watch money pour in. To a true professional businessman that would be boring anyway. He wants the contact and excitement of making money. It is just the way he keeps score!

Our economy is based on the profit system. The professional businessman plans to make a profit. He plans how he will make it. He also plans how much he wants to make.

Too few of us do that. Yet it is an integral part of being professional. How can you know how *hard* and *long* to work unless you have a goal? How will you know when you have attained your goal unless you set one?

> *The magic figure for wealth in our country is a million dollars. Every truly professional small businessman should set at least one million dollars as his goal. Not merely for the $, but for the score.*

Choosing a goal will help you attain it. This is done with sales projections, production quotas, financial planning, budgets, and guts. Why not set a personal objective?

It is surprisingly easy for a really professional small businessman who plans to make a million, to do so. A million today is not all that much. Around the turn of the century, J. P. Morgan bailed the U.S. government out of a financial crisis. No one could do that today. A million is still a good goal, however. When you reach it, you will be so active and having such fun you will not even notice it. It will be on paper and you will not be able to see it or touch it. You will probably just keep going toward your second million, if you are a pro.

The Time Is Right

Never in history have the chances to become a millionaire been better. Our economy is so vast there is plenty of room for large numbers of us to amass fortunes. There probably is not much opportunity in horseshoes and other obsolete or dying markets. (Although that may be a deceptive example, because with more leisure time available more people may take up horses as a hobby. There may be enough of them to constitute a special market—too small for big business but perfect for small business. Small business often finds its customer in unlikely or overlooked places.)

And pro small businessmen are doing just that. Although there are no official records that provide an exact count of millionaires, the Federal Reserve Board is able to deduce fairly reliable statistics from tax returns and surveys. In 1966 the estimated number of millionaires was 100,000. In mid-1987 the Federal Reserve Board estimated the number of American millionaires was 1,000,000. That's over 40,000 new millionaires a year! Nearly all are from small businesses.

The Internal Revenue Service reports that in 1984, anyone with an income of $75,000 a year or more was in the top 1% of the population. Estimating the current population at 240 million, 2.4 million people belong in this category. Since 1 million Americans are millionaires, two out of every five people in the top income group are millionaires. Why shouldn't you be one?

Perhaps the most striking comparison is this: In the 1880s and 90s, when the famous millionaires were compiling their fortunes, the GNP was around $50 billion. In

1985 the Defense Department budget alone was $265 billion annually. The total production of goods and services in 1984 was 73 times as great as in 1880. That averages out to 7% growth each year, and a doubling of total output every ten years. If a person just keeps up with this growth, he gets ahead rapidly. If he is an entrepreneur, a professional businessman, the chances are he will make his million.

It is easier now than *ever* before.

Small Business Is How

How did these new millionaires make their money? Overwhelmingly in independent small businesses. One reason is that it is almost impossible to make a million working for someone else in today's tax situation. Capital gains, not salaries, made these men and women wealthy.

Income tax statistics illustrate this fact. In 1958, 115,000 returns showed incomes of $50,000 or more. Less than 23,000 listed incomes of $100,000 or more. Yet, 40,000 of these taxpayers were, in fact, millionaires. Obviously they were not making it in salaries. Salaries do not make many millionaires.

In other words, you cannot get to be a millionaire working for someone else. But you never could. Rockefeller, Carnegie, Vanderbilt, Harriman, Duke—they did not work for someone else. They inherited it. This rules out big business for the aspiring millionaire.

Another heartening fact about past and present millionaires is that most of them start with little or nothing and make it themselves. How do they do it?

First, they work hard, put in long hours—10 to 15

hours a day, nights, weekends, especially in the beginning. Most small businessmen have to do that anyway. You already have mastered the first step.

Second, they launch their enterprises in a small market that needs improving and which may grow to be a big market—although that is not necessary. Even small markets today are big ones. Opportunities are found where problems are. The new millionaires find an economic need and fill it.

Fifty to 100 years ago fortunes were made in large basic industries—steel, power, autos. Those markets belong now to big business, having grown so huge only huge companies can serve them. Today new services, technology, or even a franchise are more likely paths to a million. As science makes more and more new discoveries, the work of the scientists, as well as the products, must be organized and developed. As people have more time free from their jobs, recreation will grow. As our population gets younger and younger—half of all Americans are now under 25—services or products for youth must grow. These are just three areas of sure growth in which many small markets exist, perfect for exploitation by an independent entrepreneur in a small business.

Third, and most important, the new millionaires can channel their wealth into capital gains situations where it can accrue to *them* rather than the IRS. This means most of their assets will never be in cash but in company ownership, real estate, and other nonliquid vehicles. When they need more cash than such holdings can pay in salaries and dividends, they have to borrow on their holdings or even sell something. But only when they sell do they pay tax on the basic source of their wealth, and then it is at the lower capital gains rate. Meanwhile, their holdings go right on appreciating without annual taxation.

This is so obvious it should not need mentioning. Yet so few businessmen follow this principle that their education must be incomplete. Millionaires do it. That is how they get that way. Which raises the question, can you learn to be a millionaire?

The Education of a Millionaire

Or the lack of it. Many of the new millionaires have sketchy formal educations. Those who have struck it rich in scientific or technological fields tend to have had more formal training. But even some of the self-made electronics tycoons never obtained college diplomas. Sixteen of the 35 wealthiest men in the U.S. did not have college degrees.

The personal stories of these men and women, recounted in numerous articles and books, prove that if you can learn to be a reasonably adept professional small businessman you can teach yourself to be a millionaire. Formal education is unnecessary.

College may be helpful but it can be a deterrent. All too many schools of higher learning are turning out graduates like cigarettes from a production machine. "*So* round, *so* firm and *so* fully packed." Even the specialists conform to a pattern. They dress alike, talk alike, look alike, and think alike. Any natural born leadership qualities are smothered.

Moreover, colleges and business schools today are geared to turn out personnel for big business. Few curricula of the graduate business schools teach much about small business or individual entrepreneurism. Many college graduates look down their noses at business per se, and especially at starting from scratch under trying conditions. Liberal arts courses frequently turn out dreamy misfits. Professors are breeding more professors. Technical courses create narrow specialists with expensive research tastes who often are not willing to make the initial sacrifices of small business. College graduates, up until recently, were so hotly wooed by big business that most of their heads are turned by the immediate salaries, cushy fringe benefits, and lifetime security. Colleges today prepare you to work for someone else; millionaires are not made that way.

We hear a lot about college dropouts today but little is being said about college men *dropping out* of big business. Business schools today are preparing their students to go into big business. Naturally, for it is from big business that they get their annual endowments! It is big business which sends teams of recruiters to each college each spring, with large expense accounts, lavish hotel suites, booze, etcetera. If you must go into big business, become a recruiter. Big business knows this, and studies indicate that big business hires five guys to get one. This is an unfair big business practice. The professors will not tell, of course; big business will not tell either. So, five fair-haired boys go to work for Generous Electric and a very few years later only one of those five is still there. The other four are "dropouts."

These "dropouts" are not too useful to your small business, because first, they are spoiled by the high salaries originally offered. Second, they are spoiled by big company organization and management. Third, very little of what they learned while there is of any value to your small business.

The non-college grad often tries harder because he

thinks he has to. No big corporation is out bidding for him, at least not at the executive level. This gives him a terrific competitive advantage. He has the will to succeed and the willingness to back it up with work. He is not likely to feel any tasks are beneath his dignity.

Whether or not you went to college is, therefore, a minor consideration in succeeding as a professional small businessman and making your million. The educated guy often grows soft and reflective; the nongraduate is out hustling to prove what he can do.

Incredible Opportunity Ahead

Between 1966 and 1986 the GNP increased from $743 billion to over $4 trillion, a gain of $3.3 trillion or over 444%. Millionnaires in this period increased from 100,000 to nearly 1,000,000, a gain of 900,000 or 900%. The number of millionaires grew twice as fast as the GNP. If the increase in millionaires only keeps pace with the growth in the GNP, 100,000 new millionaires a year will be made during the years ahead.

Will you be one of them? Can you teach yourself to join their ranks? The facts about the new millionaires prove that learning to be a professional small businessman *is* learning to become a millionaire. Think about it. You must first learn how to keep score!

CHAPTER XVI

How to Make
a Million
Through Promiscuity

LET's assume you have made the commitment toward business professionalism. You have seen the wisdom of owning your own business. And you have started one which is now relatively successful. At least it is a going concern.

You are at a crucial point. Beware!

Don't fall in love with your business!

You can slip right back out of professionalism into artisanry by falling in love with your initial field of endeavor, like a proud parent fondly surveying his firstborn.

A businessman should be pleased with progress. But you must be even more concerned that it does not overwhelm you, lull you to apathy. Damaging things happen when you have a romance with one particular business.

It breeds inability to delegate authority. You love the company so much that you want no competing suitors waiting on her. Fear or lack of confidence could not wreck management communication more effectively.

It kills objectivity and fosters emotional decisions. Stupid things occur, like building castles for company offices.

Falling in love with one company steals time the professional businessman could use to start a new venture. Or to make extra profit from other businesses he has.

All of these stifle subordinates. They lose confidence in the boss and wonder if they are with the right company.

It makes the owner a slave to the business. He cannot enjoy the freedom which is the hallmark of a well-run business because he has not delegated authority to others who can take over in his absence. You cannot sell a business to which the owner is a slave. It has considerably less value than a similar company with identical volume and profit, but which has professional management.

It is too easy to sit at your desk shuffling papers—it is habit-forming. Or hang around making employees miserable by nagging on minor points because you fear something bad is going to happen. That is not professional conduct. Nor is it freedom for you or for them.

Freedom to play golf must be differentiated from the freedom to start a new business. If a man's only interest is getting out to play, freedom is wasted on him—though even that is preferable to shuffling papers. New businesses have unusual potential for the pro businessman. They can make capital gains much faster than the owner's established business. It is easier for a new company to go from $100,000 volume to $1 million than for the established firm to go from one million to five, providing you still want to own it.

The best way to avoid falling in love with one business is to have more than one.

The question is *when* to start business No. 2? Many of us are struggling to make our first one successful. Should we go out and start No. 2?

Which comes first for the professional businessman: Having more than one business? Or the ability to run any small business professionally?

When to Start Business No. 2

Before starting a second business, be sure your original company can operate without you. Or with you there only part-time. If you are not sure there is an easy way to find out. Go away for a while. It may take only a week to find out how the company can do without you. Or it may take six months.

This technique has the double value of testing the entrepreneur to be sure he is not in love with business No. 1. If you can live without being involved in the detail of running it, you may be ready to start No. 2. If you discover you are in love with your business the time away will separate the lover from the object of his affections and may help break up the romance.

Being faithful to one may be fine for marriage but it is bad for building your future. Businesses do not reproduce the way people do. Promiscuity is a byword for success in business.

To be a professional small businessman you must be promiscuous.

If you have built one successful small business, do not push it (and yourself) against the tide. Get a good manager, train him thoroughly, watch him carefully . . . and go out and start another business. When No. 2 is similarly successful, do it all over again. When you are spending much of your time with your lawyer and accountants figuring tax savings and estate planning, you will be a pro. The most successful kind.

The first step on that road may be the vacation you take to see whether your initial business can run by itself. If it can, that is assurance you can delegate authority. It will also indicate that you have chosen capable people.

The best thing about this method is even if it develops that you have more building to do at old No. 1 before plunging into No. 2, you will be rested from your vacation and ready to make the necessary changes so the company *can* run by itself. If it turns out that you are ready to tackle No. 2, you will be rested for that.

By the time you are thinking of starting your second business (or third, fourth or fifth) you will deserve a vacation anyway.

Preparing for the time away and announcing it has a drama all its own. When the plans are laid, call a meeting.

"You men are doing a splendid job. I am needed less and less so I am going to Florida for a few weeks for a vacation."

Later they will get to thinking of the changes your being away will cause. They see it as a chance for advancement. Your absence puts the responsibility squarely on them. They appreciate the compliment of your confidence. What higher compliment can you give?

But—do leave a phone number.

Your executives may be able to solve any situation themselves without having to call the boss long distance to say, "I need help." This handling of ultimate responsibility helps men grow.

One day, sooner or later, your phone will ring.

"Hi, Boss. Pete. How's the weather down there?"

"Beautiful. Eighty in the shade. How is it there?"

"Terrible! Worst winter in a long time. You sure picked the right one to go South.

"Guess you're right. It's great here."

Finally, Pete begins. "Something just came up that I

thought you would be interested in." Note that he carefully avoided saying, "I need help."

He will spill out some problem, or more likely some statistical data presented "for your information." But it will be a minor problem, one you know—and he knows—he is fully capable of handling. Or some data which you are accustomed to receiving from him or which he feels will be a pleasant surprise. More chitchat will follow, and probably another compliment on your superb judgment in picking just the right winter to go to Florida.

The conversation seems about to end. You are beginning to wonder why he bothered calling. Casually, seemingly an afterthought, Pete will then say: "Oh, by the way . . ." Look out! Here comes the real thing worrying Pete. The prior conversation was simply an excuse for calling. He did not want to have to call you to ask for help so he put *himself* in the role of a friendly helper and passed along some things he knew would interest you, usually good news.

You have to be especially alert when away. Listen carefully to inflections of the voice. Watch who calls, what about, how often. This gives you the true test of your men.

Probably you will detect some conflicts. Jockeying for position may get underway.

Such conflicts are good! Especially at this time, since the reason you went away was to discover what conditions will be like when you are absent regularly. Many times this trial absence will enable the staff to get all the pent-up jealousy and animosity out of their systems. By the time you return they will have decided they like working together after all. Maybe the opposite. Whatever happens you need to know how things really stand before launching No. 2, and your vacation will most likely tell you. While you are there it will not hurt if you do soak up some of that sun.

Tips and Tactics

Do not start a second business to run away from unsolved problems in your first. Better to sell it and start a different No. 1. Do not start No. 2 because you are bored with No. 1, unless it is successful enough to stand by itself. Then you have reason to be bored. Running away from business problems is not the object of a second business.

If you need a divorce from No. 1, get one. Then get remarried to a new No. 1 you can live with. As in private life, analyze yourself and the object of your affection intensively before divorcing. It may be a good and necessary thing but it may be a big mistake. Think of the time and effort you have put into your initial marriage (business). If there is any way you can make it go on its own, under a manager, chances are overwhelming that you will be better off. You, yourself, may have been stifling this business for years and not been aware of it.

The "promiscuous" analogy might easily be termed the "polygamy" approach. As soon as one business family is happily and profitably established, go out and find another sweetheart and start a second family. Like the Arabian sheiks, the more you have the better off you will be.

Sometimes small business has to start really small. The first "plant" may be a garage, basement shop, or single room. This is also true of a second business, or should be. You do not need one square foot of extra space since presumably you are already well housed in your first place of business. Do not be afraid to start your second business small, just as you did your first.

Because they are successful with one company, some businessmen feel they have to keep up their image when they branch out. They go real-estate-wild and equipment-happy, fitting out the second business as if it were already a great success. This is a waste of money—money the second business will need when it encounters rough going, as most every company does.

Delegating Authority

If a pharmacist has one drugstore which he runs personally, he is a druggist. If he has two stores, he is half a druggist and half a businessman. By the time he gets three or more stores he is a businessman employing several pharmacists. His time is spent tending to business decisions, not filling prescriptions.

The professional businessman, once he learns a job, hires others to do what he has learned. He then expands his abilities and knowledge. When he has mastered another step he hires or promotes others to do that. Ad infinitum.

That's the rub. Some human beings, however talented, are failures at delegating authority and providing leadership. More than any other reason this keeps them from becoming professional businessmen and gaining the success open to them. If you have this problem, face it. You might as well, because as soon as you start No. 2 it will face you. No man can run two businesses, even really small ones, without relying on others.

Techniques of leadership and delegating authority can be learned. Another way of solving this problem is to take in a partner or large stockholder. That may come up of its own accord when you are ready to start a second business, since additional capital may be needed, or special skills. Instead of hiring someone to whom you must provide leadership, it may suit your purpose to join with another person on the ownership level. If you find it difficult to delegate authority, team up with someone whose strength is just that. You concentrate on your highest skill level and let him be the administrator, the delegator of authority.

In this way a person who is essentially an artisan can make his million too. And even have a second, third, or fourth small business. He can hire or join with a professional businessman. The two skills—artisanship and business acumen—will make a strong unit.

Income Mix

That a businessman should have more than one business may be a new idea to some small businessmen. The soundness of this has its financial benefits.

Expense accounts are one example. This is an area increasingly scrutinized by Internal Revenue. It is generally permissible, however, for a company to own a car for use in the business and to pay business expenses through an expense account. If you have one company, this is what you can deduct. If you have five companies, multiply some of these advantages by five.

If you have one small company it can maybe afford one company car for the owner.

One bigger company can have one bigger car.

If you have two companies you may be able to have two deductible cars. Maybe a plane, or a boat, too.

Three companies may offer two cars, a plane and a boat.

Four companies, two cars, a plane, a boat and a camp. For entertaining customers, of course.

Five companies put you in the same class as big businessmen who may enjoy several cars, a jet aircraft, a yacht, and a mistress! (It is very difficult to deduct the latter, however, and if you could, your alimony payments would not make it worthwhile.)

Expense account jokes are not as frequent as they used to be. The IRS is catching up. More businesses will provide you with more *legitimate* expenses.

More important, if you have two or three businesses you can take two or three salaries. Two or three expense accounts are better than one, but two or three salaries are even better still—and with several companies you can have some of both.

Multiple salaries, coming from several businesses, stabilize and strengthen your income by distributing it over a broader base. A poor year in one business cannot hurt you as much.

Such income mix makes sense for the businessman just as it does for his companies. A large company avoids having all its sales come from one product. It diversifies its product line, or product mix. Why not follow the same procedure with your income mix? This is reason why you should not fall in love with one business.

Why Capital Gains Makes Wealth and Cash Does Not

Some people think the way to make money is to build up a big bank account. Professional businessmen have learned the only way to really make money is through capital gains, through building net worth, not cash.

The man who makes his million today *cannot* make money in the form of cash. If he does, most of it will be lost in taxes. Cash is taxed as soon as it is taken out of a business. It can be banked or lent at only 8% to 10% interest, which itself is also taxed.

Building wealth is a matter of building equity. Cash burns a hole in your pocket. Capital gains cannot because it is not in your pocket or your checking account. Cash is valueless unless you put it to work as capital. Continuing inflation makes cash *worth less* each year.

It is the capital gains potential of having more than one business that is most valuable For if two or three salaries and expense accounts are better than one how much more so are two or three capital gains potentials better than one.

· I know several relatively unsuccessful small businessmen who think in terms of how many Standard Oil shares they own. Is this a hedge against their own business inability? Or is it a status symbol? Why do they invest in other, bigger companies?

Though such men may not be professional small businessmen. their action admits to the wisdom of not falling in love with one business. By purchasing stocks they too are diversifying.

But this is not the vigorous, confident, forward-looking activity of the pro. Why invest in someone else's business, whether Ford Motors or some local concern, when you can invest in your own? If it is because you can make more profit in someone else's company, you had better sell yours at once!

In someone else's business you have no control of management. In your own business, complete control is yours. It reflects lack of confidence, to say the least, when a businessman invests heavily or primarily in other companies, unless there are substantial modifying circumstances.

The satisfaction of building your own companies through personal investment far outweigh watching stock quotations in the daily paper.

Most important, the income potential to you in your own successful business is way beyond what stock in the brightest blue chip or fastest-growing public company can offer. Capital gains appreciation, expense accounts, tax advantages, estate planning—what stock ever paid dividends to equal these, even if your business is only modestly successful?

This is not to suggest that buying stocks, or even bonds, is not good. As part of an overall investment program it may be wise diversification. But if your investments are that extensive you either made a bundle by the very techniques suggested here or your rich uncle left you one. The man on the way up, the professional businessman, will have very little money available to invest in anyone else's business.

To make his million he will diversify his holdings by starting additional small businesses. He will be promiscuous, loving business in general rather than any particular one.

Real Estate

The most logical second business is real estate. Your original company has to be housed, so why not form a real estate holding company to provide it?

There are several types of real estate business. *A brokerage* is a sales agency which has little or no capital gains potential. You may want to get a brokerage license for convenience but it is more profitable to employ it as an *entrepreneur* buying and selling properties of your own. This has good capital gains possibilities. *Land development* offers great capital gains if you have the capital to make the gains possible.

Entrepreneurism and land development are wheeling and dealing operations not for the faint-hearted. They have been highly touted as get-rich-quick opportunities. Remember the best seller, *How I Turned $1,000 into $3 Million in Real Estate—in My Spare Time?*

For the small businessman starting a second company, such fancy ideas should be kept at arm's length. So must the arrangements between your original business and your real estate company, unless you want to qualify for IRS investigation.

Here are some advantages of a real estate company:

1. Your company writes off rent or upkeep anyway. Why not channel some of that money into your personal pocket? Money spent by your company on leasehold improvements is deductible and also improves the value of the property *you* own through your real estate company.
2. During bad periods *your* real estate company can allow your business to skip or fall behind on rent.
3. The lessee can pay taxes, insurance, and all expenses including maintenance. They are deductible. The holding company's investment and cash needs are reduced to almost nothing by this method.
4. Land is limited in quantity. People are multiplying unprecedentedly. Competition for land use is pushing

values higher and higher. Under these circumstances, the only way real estate prices can go is up.

5. Land is an inflationary safeguard. Its value rises proportionately to inflation and population. And because God isn't making any more.

6. You can buy real estate for less cash outlay than most things. Mortgages up to 60 or even 80% are available and this is *long-term* money.

7. Payments on mortgages are not payments at all. They are forced savings since they build your equity. Excepting the interest, you are paying the money to yourself. This makes real estate mortgages a good way to be certain you use your funds to build your net worth, and the interest is deductible against your other income.

8. Real estate lends itself to all kinds of tax savings, cash-raising, investment, and trading angles. It offers wide leeway to suit your particular tax problems, investment needs, or capital requirements. You can do a lot of wheeling and dealing with real estate.

9. Real estate is the best possible collateral. Even banks accept it without reservation.

These advantages are multiplied when your company acquires additional property to lease to others.

In addition to capital gains, real estate saves you taxes through depreciation. This one-two punch allows you to deduct the *cost* of real estate as depreciation, then retain most of the property's *appreciation* as capital gains when you sell. These are both complicated tax matters requiring special study or professional assistance. But Uncle Sam and inflation can almost buy real estate for you if you handle it properly.

However, contrary to suggestions outlined in Chapter II, real estate is the one business that *must not* be incorporated. Recent tax laws require that all profits from a real estate sale be taxed as ordinary income and *not* capital gains. Here again, advice of professionals should be sought.

Once the real estate company is established by owning the building which houses your original business it is ready to look elsewhere for property to develop. Unlike manufacturing or retailing, this is a business which need not take much of your time but silently, over the years, may substantially increase your net worth. The time left over can be spent in starting your third business.

Service Businesses

A professional businessman can make money in any business. Once it is established he will employ others to perform the work detail while he manages. This will pyramid his income and allow free time in which to start another business.

A real estate broker, for example, profits by sales made for him by his sales staff. His part of the deal is to provide the executive ability, sales management, offices, telephones, advertising, clerical help, and a brokerage license. He need not be on hand all the time in order to profit.

But there is no capital gains opportunity by which his profit can compound itself through appreciation.

For this reason, most service businesses are of little interest to the professional businessman. If you have a special skill or training, a service business may be your route to Company No. 1. You will need to progress into Company No. 2, however, to obtain the objectives of the professional businessman (capital gains, etcetera).

In the case of real estate, most progressive brokers are

also entrepreneurs or land developers. This does constitute two businesses but is less desirable because both are in the same industry. If real estate suffers temporarily, they take a double rap.

Other service businesses, such as insurance agencies, product or commodity brokers, sales agencies or travel agencies, have small capital gains possibilities. Their only advantage is that you are self-employed rather than working for someone else.

This makes you a small businessman by definition. If you are a professional you will start a second business as soon as possible.

Some types of service businesses offer capital gain's opportunities. Resort entertainment and restaurant establishments often realize substantial appreciation, though most of it is through the increase in the value of the location and the real estate. Contract service businesses which have a wide market with a recurring need and long term contracts can provide good net appreciation possibilities. Background music service, telephone answering service, fire and burglar alarm service are in this group, to name a few. The best businesses in this category are usually franchises.

Retailing

So diverse is the retailing field, and so specialized, that retailers tend to think it unusually complicated. Actually it is simple in theory and operation. Sales complications arise from the lack of specialized product knowledge necessary to the community.

You must be a businessman first and a specialty man second. Like many small businessmen, retailers often reverse the order, becoming jewelers or fashion experts primarily and businessmen inadvertently.

Retailing is a service business. The mounting complaints about poor service and discourteous clerks—to say nothing of the almost total absence of *sales* personnel in place of mere clerks—suggest most retailers have forgotten this basic fact. They have become narrow specialists in one type of merchandise or another whose attitude, as sensed by their complaining customers, is that the public somehow owes them its patronage.

The universality of complaints about retailers has created a great opportunity for anyone who opens a store which demonstrates that customers come first.

Retailing is a service business because it usually does no manufacturing itself but offers the service of a convenient place to buy products of several manufacturers. A dramatic example of the diversity of merchandise modern retailers must cope with is cited by Samuel Feinberg in his *Women's Wear Daily* column. Quoting the president of a Midwestern department store, Feinberg points out that ten years ago the buyer in the lingerie department had to worry about 750 items of stock. These were comprised of 50 sizes in 5 types, 95% of which were in white with the remainder split between just two other colors.

Because of changing fashion due to greater affluence and a growing, better-educated population, that same buyer today allots only 50% of her total stock to white merchandise, splits the remainder between at least a dozen other colors, including prints, keeps 65 sizes in 12 types and has 5 stores to look after instead of one—making a grand total of 50,700 items of stock! In ten years this buyer's stock control problem has grown by 49,950 items.

Under such circumstances there is no denying the complexity of day-to-day details in retailing. But every business has its operational complications, which are no excuse for not being a professional businessman first and a detail specialist second.

Even the food store owner is not exempt from this sales psychology—as a visit to the supermarket will convince you. Small food stores illustrate how much retailing has become a service business. They cannot hope to compete with the giant supermarket chains on price or selection. Yet every town still has many small food stores, new specialty franchises, cheese shops, etcetera. They survive because of the service they offer. Being open at all hours, neighborhood location, specializing in certain types of foods, perhaps offering credit, delivering.

If you are contemplating opening a retail store there are several organizations and publications to guide you. It is foolish to enter any business without thorough research but especially so in retailing.

What is the future of the small store? Jane Cahill, for 15 years a specialist on the subject, sums it up in her book, *Can a Smaller Store Succeed?*

> The future of the smaller store lies in remaining small. There are thousands of big stores for customers to shop in so why try to compete? Better to set up a unique smaller store operation supplying selective specific consumer needs and stick to it.

Proof of her theory is that a huge department store is nothing more than a collection of many smaller stores. The big stores spend millions every year trying to create exclusivity and an intimate atmosphere. A small store has these to start with.

Miss Cahill's advice makes sense for all types of small business, not just retailing.

The Safe Shortcut of a Franchise

Anyone who still thinks there is no opportunity today should read the "Franchises Available" column of the *Wall Street Journal* or the "Business Opportunities" in any large newspaper. One company's ad copy epitomizes both the opportunity and the special way franchising makes it available:

Franchise Offerings   *Franchise Offerings*

SORRY, the first 450 Midas Muffler Shops are gone! If you wait much longer, these prime markets may not be available either; Waterbury, Conn., Philadelphia, Charleston, S.C., Savannah, Huntington, Cincinnati, Nashville, Little Rock, Binghamton and Harrisburg, plus other choice locations throughout the country, including California.

AS A MIDAS DEALER:
Your market today is over 70 million automobiles and it's growing yearly.

Your products are mufflers, pipes and related exhaust system parts, shock absorbers, smog-control systems and more to come from bumper to bumper.

Your profit margins and return on invested capital are unusually high compared to say industry and business of any size. And MIDAS provides locations and builds shops for franchises.

Your security is with the franchise company that is financially sound, more than a quarter of a century old, but with young, ambitious ideas for its own and its dealers' future.

Your role is one of a businessman, active in all facets

of your business, merchandising, management and selling. You are not a garageman, mechanic or clerk.

Learn about MIDAS from the Midas dealer in your city. Or, ask your banker or stock broker, or anyone who has bought a MIDAS Muffler (they're usually impressed). Cash investment range is $15,000 to $25,000. There is no charge for the franchise.

For further details write—

MIDAS
MUFFLER
SHOPS

The above ad also points up a problem. In bigger cities most of the better franchises are taken. The small towns are still wide open, however—and small towns and small business were made for each other.

Franchises make big brand names available to small businessmen. Restaurants, drive-ins, ice cream stands, automatic laundries, car washes, auto paint, repairs and accessory shops, hotels, motels, donut shops, family recreation centers—these and many other types of businesses are franchised. *You* can be running a Howard Johnson's, Holiday Inn, Sheraton Hotel, Muzak®, Westinghouse Laundromat, Rayco, Dunkin' Donut, Dairy Queen or McDonald's, and a host of others through franchising.

The parent company does nearly everything to set up your business for you. After you make the down payment some will even finance you. They profit from royalties, fees, or selling you their products for resale, so they can only do as much business as you do. It is in their interest to help you become as successful as possible.

These companies are very thorough and professional in helping you get established. They will help you choose the location, based on research and testing. Even though you may own a piece of land at another location, they will not give you the franchise unless you locate it in the spot their experts know will be best. Once land is purchased, they help design and construct the building. furnish it, train you, hire the help, do the advertising, set up the bookkeeping, even steer you away from costly errors their experience has taught them to avoid.

Franchising has grown so big it has its own trade associations. It has become an important enough segment of the business world that Boston College recently opened a Center for the Study of Franchise Distribution.

Despite their recent prominence, franchises are not new. Most automobile dealerships and service stations are franchises.

Everything from vending machines to hotels are franchised today. Several fascinating volumes could be written about success stories in this field, many of whose pioneers are still young men.

A franchise might be called an instant business. *Just add capital and open.*

A franchise is particularly suitable for your Company No. 2.

What about capital gains? How do franchisers measure up on this yardstick? Because there are replicas of your franchise in locations across the country, and because all of them together constitute a Big Company with a famous, nationally advertised brand name, franchises overcome capital gains disadvantages of most small service and retail businesses. As the brand name grows the value of each franchise can increase.

What is more, a franchise is one of the few businesses

not publicly held *which constantly reveals its saleable value*. By collecting operating statistics from each franchisee, parent companies establish an accepted selling price for established units. Often it is a multiple of monthly sales volume. Each month, twelve times a year, you know the worth of your business. This figure may have little or no relationship with your financial statements.

Nationally it may be that the average franchise of your type sells for 25 times its monthly billing. If your sales are $10,000 per month, you can be reasonably confident the business could be sold for $250,000. Some nationally known franchises have buyers waiting in line.

If your franchise operation is sloppy and your equipment ill-cared-for, naturally a purchaser will pay less. If your franchise is exceptionally strong, you may get more. The point is this, as opposed to the average nonaffiliated business, a franchise has an established market price. It is like comparing stock in an unlisted company with a listed one. Because the listed stock is traded regularly, a market exists which establishes the price. The same is nearly true of a franchise. There are guidelines for buying a business in any industry, usually a ratio of profit, income, or market potential. Guidelines are much stronger, however, with a nationally known franchise.

Often the franchiser will find a buyer for you if you decide to sell. Quality control is their stock in trade since a poor operator can drag down the reputation of the entire chain. This almost forces the franchiser to supervise the sale of your franchise to protect his name and quality. Therefore, the better-managed franchises are very liquid. You can get your money out fast.

SBA recognizes this by its liberal loan policies for franchise operations. When the SBA Administrator, Bernard

L. Boutin, announced these policies in late 1966, it was estimated there were 400,000 franchised outlets in existence. Since then the field has mushroomed at a dizzying pace, to a total of 529,000 outlets in 1985.

Entrepreneurs and promoters ought to be more concerned with franchising.

When you are ready to branch out, talk to several franchise representatives, even if you are not particularly interested. Whether or not you decide to obtain one, the discussions will help focus your thinking on what type of business you do want to open as Company No. 2.

Industry Mix

By the same reasoning that product mix and income mix are sought, industry mix should be considered in opening additional businesses. The stockbroker whose second business is investing in the stock market is concentrating his hopes in a single industry. He is doubly vulnerable.

Measure yourself as part of the decision. What do you like to do best? What is your experience? Your successes? Failures? Professional businessmen are objective about which industries they enter but not cold blooded. You do your best at something you like.

A professional businessman starting his second or third business has advantages over someone starting his initial company. To the man starting Company No. 1 these may appear more substantial than they are, however. The basic income from one going business cannot be denied its importance. Or the experience of having made that company successful. The staff assembled and contacts made among suppliers, bankers and others should also be helpful in establishing Company No. 2.

But there are disadvantages. Too often overconfidence creeps in. Because a businessman has made one company go he is sure he can make any business succeed. This has a certain logic but is not necessarily true. He may under-value the cautions which research for the new business uncovers, feeling his experience will see him through. He may take unwarranted financial risks, banking on the stability and assets of his original company to pull him out. He may become equipment happy or real estate prone.

The new businessman is less apt to suffer from these maladies and is advantaged thereby. He *knows* he has got to make it with the company he is starting or lose precious years and capital starting over. A businessman who can retain the feeling of urgency each time he starts a business is over halfway to success to begin with.

Someone once said you have to have the feel of bankruptcy before you ever become really successful. Isn't this exactly the feeling you had many times while struggling with your original business? Now that it is part of you, and your judgment, hold on to it securely. Let it help ensure your success the second time around.

Do not fall in love with your business . . . or your industry. Be greedy, promiscuous. Take at least two. They are small.

PART FIVE

CAUTIONARY THINKING

CHAPTER XVII

Small Business and Government Work

THE problem of the small businessman engaged in the development and manufacture of equipment for the defense program is an interesting one.

The small company today is handicapped more than ever before when doing government business. Here are some of the problems encountered with both prime and subcontract government work.

Advertised Prime Contracts

Usual government procurement policies make it very difficult for legitimate small manufacturers to obtain contracts in a legitimate way. Advertised bids are a very small percentage of the total and those that are limited to small business many times are placed at a price barely covering cost of materials. Some "loft" operators, with little responsibility, always can underbid an established firm. This results in:

.1. Contractor asking for more dollars (frequently gets it due to some loophole or inside information regarding increased quantities or spares), or,

2. Dispute arises, delaying the procurement and not helping either the government or the small business.

Negotiated Prime Contracts

There seems to be a large amount of "defense" dollars going in this direction. Small business has little chance of getting a fair share. Sometimes it takes weeks to complete negotiations which require lawyers, engineers, and accountants on both sides. Mr. Small's company cannot afford this expense even if it *were* an allowable cost on the contract! The big firms maintain a staff in Washington for this purpose. Legal and illegal five-percenters do help in many cases but their association with a small firm is usually short-lived. Legitimate sales representatives cannot afford the time that is required to service every small contract.

Mr. Small's company is usually faced with taking some research and development work as part of the package, or getting no contract at all. Research and development for Mr. Small has further pitfalls.

He does not have adequate personnel or equipment that the proposal really required.

Because his staff is limited in size and ability, the government experts usually make a better deal for the government with Mr. Small than they would be able to make with a large concern. Colleges, universities and other nonprofit institutions now become his competitors in the research and development field. Although he can underbid them, and frequently does, due to his ingenuity, it is obvious that research and development can usually be better accomplished by a large staff with all facilities in either an institution endowed for the purpose or a large firm.

Larger companies have other advantages on research and development over Mr. Small's company. For example, they can afford to lose dollars on R & D and make it up on production. Usually the firm that develops the equipment is in a very strong position to *negotiate* for the production when it comes along.

The large firms have extreme tax advantages over Mr. Small. Chances are that they are making plenty of money on commercial products. They are aware that some government research and development business *looks* good in their annual report. Even if they lose money year after year on this work it only costs them $.50 while Mr. Small's losses amount to $1.00. Mr. Small risks his whole company on nearly *every* government job. It can be a small job but to him it is a large percentage of his total business. If there is a "booby trap" in the specifications, or if he just "goofs," he risks *all*. Government attorneys can do nothing but follow the regulations and many times force a small company into bankruptcy. Mr. Small's attorneys are certainly no match for these experts.

Mr. Small's fee is "peanuts" even if they win the case. Mr. Small has trouble getting competent legal help versed in the complexities of government contractual red tape.

Government sub-contracts are not much better. When the prime government contractor needs to perform he sub-contracts to small businesses. This is great except when his contracts are cut back. Then watch out! Who is the first to go? You are! You have expanded your plant and suddenly Washington changes its missile (or mind) and you have had it.

Mr. Small's company usually has all of his people under one roof. His modest success has been the result of long hours, ingenuity, moving fast and improving his products in order to keep abreast of competition. He lands a government contract with some amount of engineering involved and he gradually finds he has a *new management problem*. Upon receipt of his new contract he augments his staff, hires engineers, technicians, increases his drafting department, etcetera.

The boys plugged into the government job punch out at 5 P.M. while Mr. Small and his older employees are used to ignoring the clock in order to get a job done. Friction builds up fast between government and non-government workers, pay rates have to be adjusted, overhead goes up and *even* before the contract is finished he is losing money on it. Furthermore, in order to keep the older people happy he may go a little overboard in their direction and six months later he learns that he is losing money on his regular commercial products.

Now he is in a dilemma. His accountants tell him one solution is to increase sales. So he goes out and gets another government contract. Government business has gradually taken over his plant. He loses his competitive position on his original commercial products. He, himself, is spending most of his time in government negotiations on which he must be lawyer, salesman, engineer and accountant.

The government cost people are telling him that he can only charge this and that into their contract, he is limited to 6 to 10% profit before taxes if he is lucky.

He is really frustrated. He cannot go back. His old staff (now going home promptly at 5 P.M.) with new offices, secretaries and all the trimmings, would never go back to the old days. Mr. Small's own salary and personal business expenses are now reviewed nearly every month by a government accountant. Mr. Small always prided himself on owning his own business but now he is worse off than if he had a nine-to-five job with a big corporation.

An overpaid civil servant not only knows all about his own business but is telling him how he must run it.

Mr. Small is in financial trouble too! This government business has forced him to expand beyond the capabilities of his working capital. He expanded because he had to do more volume to make the same dollar profit that he used to make. The government is frequently slow-pay due to red tape, so his bank gives him a loan (in which he has to sign his life away including his wife's property). Now *he* is "financing the government." On part of each contract he has to pay high interest.

Mr. Small used to think in terms of "it is deductible." Now he has forgotten all that. His decisions are frequently based on "is it an allowable cost on a contract?"

More contracts roll in, he spends more time with the bank, his attorneys and in Washington. He loses some of his original men because of lack of contact with them. They are now making more money at some other government-subsidized plant. The bank wants more collateral. He has a much bigger company now *but* making less money. Besides, he is not doing the things he likes to do, and does best.

Soon a large listed corporation comes along and, by printing a few more stock certificates, offers Mr. Small more money than he *now* thinks his company is worth. They frequently pay more than the company is worth but no one cares! The thousands of little stockholders think this diversification is just fine! The employment contract (really part of the purchase price) looks good to Mr. Small too!

Mr. Small decides to accept the big outfit's offer and sells his company. He buys a yacht and everyone lives happily thereafter. But what happened to that nice little profitable small business that makes up the backbone of our nation's economy?

The preceding material was first written in 1958, in response to a request from then Senator John F. Kennedy for the "views of small businessmen on the problems with which they are faced."*

Although this material was written so long ago, it has needed little updating. In 1984, however, Congress finally took legislative action to help remedy the difficulties small businesses faced in getting government contracts. First, they passed the Competition in Contracting Act (CICA), which requires federal agencies to solicit competing proposals whenever possible. A second law, the Small Business and Federal Procurement Competition and Enhancement Act, ordered the SBA to install its own team of "watchdogs" to search for ways small business contractors can help the government save money. So far, the new laws haven't torn the government from the embrace of prime contractors, but you'd be wise to monitor developments in this area.

What often happens is that a company becomes so dependent on government work it cannot get along without it. In order to borrow money needed to keep going while

---

* Sen. John F. Kennedy's answer indicated he was aware of this problem. He wrote the author: "I do not think you should feel any hesitancy in trying to publish (the article), at least from the standpoint of its being strongly worded for strong words are sometimes needed to penetrate hidebound thinking."

waiting payment for the first contract companies are forced
to get another contract. As soon as they get a second
one they borrow as much as possible only to find, like a
check kiter, that when payment for the first one finally
arrives it is insufficient to take up the slack caused by
unexpected expenses of getting or performing the second
contract. The solution is often to get a third contract.

What this amounts to is contract kiting. It is fine as long
as contracts keep coming. But when they fall off the result
is the same as kiting checks. Bankruptcy and/or jail and
thousands of Ph.D.'s, engineers and technicians suddenly
are unemployed.

Before you start courting the bureaucrats for government contracts, think it over carefully.

CHAPTER XVIII

Estate Planning

In 1982 Congress gave small business owners—and their families—a tremendous gift by greatly liberalizing the estate tax laws. Previously, heirs to an estate—including the surviving spouse—owed tax on every dollar over $60,000. Today, however, estates worth a whopping $600,000 or less are not subject to any estate tax. Furthermore, all property passing to the surviving spouse, no matter how much, is exempt from all federal estate taxes.

This new law may bring you a great sense of relief, but it doesn't mean that you can ignore estate planning, for two reasons. First, most states have inheritance taxes, and a significant number have yet to follow the lead of the federal government by easing tax bites that can take a significant chunk of your estate. Second, and most important, your business could well be so successful that your estate will be worth more than $600,000. Although your spouse won't suffer from your lack of planning, your children and grandchildren could pay a heavy price—between 37% and 55% of your estate, over $600,000.

Estate planning should be on your mind from the first day you start your own business. You should block out time to thoroughly discuss estate planning with your spouse (and perhaps with your children or other heirs),

then confer with your banker, lawyer, or other experts
when the time comes to structure your affairs. It is not
the intention here to go into detail, but there are a few
things worth mentioning that might at least stimulate some
questions when you sit down with your estate planner,
banker, lawyer, or life insurance agent.

You should begin by considering the advantages of
giving away money while you're still alive. The gift tax
law has been greatly liberalized. You can now give away
$10,000 a year—$20,000 if you're married and your
spouse consents—to any person, without paying gift tax.
Over a number of years, such gifts—in cash, stock in your
company, real estate, or other assets—can remove a substantial sum from your estate. The only disadvantage to
such gifts is that the recipient must pay the steeper new
rates on capital gains upon selling any appreciated property, such as stocks or bonds.

More favorable tax treatment under the 1986 Tax
Reform Act is accorded life insurance. Dividends and interest that accrue on a policy are not taxable as income or
capital gains unless the policy is surrendered. The one
thing you must remember about life insurance is that after
your death, the proceeds of the policy are not considered
part of your estate if the beneficiary is your spouse, but
they *are* considered part of your estate if the beneficiary
is anyone else. The way to avoid their taxation is to "give"
the policy to the beneficiary, making him the owner of the
plan. You continue to make the premium payments, and
cash value builds up without current tax liability to the
owner. A caution: consult with a knowledgeable insurance
agent and a good tax lawyer ahead of time—the premium
payments under some circumstances may be treated by

the IRS as falling under the $10,000 (or $20,000) annual gift limit.

A third point to ponder, if your estate is going to exceed $600.000, is to be wary about joint ownership of assets with your spouse. Let us assume that your estate totals $1.2 million, and all property is jointly owned. When you die, your spouse is automatically sole owner of the $1.2 million. But when he dies, $600,000 of the estate is taxable to the heirs.

One excellent way to avoid this problem is for a husband and wife to divide all property equally. Each spouse should then leave the property in trust, with the income going to the surviving spouse during his or her lifetime, then the principal passing to the heirs upon the death of the surviving spouse. Using such a trust arrangement, both husband and wife can pass on $600,000 to their heirs, free of federal estate taxes.

Keep the above ideas in mind when you discuss planning with your banker, lawyer, accountant, insurance agent, and other experts. Unfortunately, you are going to have to rely on them for advice. The many fine books and other publications on estate planning became largely useless upon passage of the 1986 Tax Reform Law. It's going to be years until definitive books are written to replace them, for two reasons. First, tax experts believe that Congress will tinker with the provisions of the tax laws for the next few years after gauging the effects on federal revenues. Secondly, the exact effects of many provisions will change after these provisions are tested in front of the tax commission and the courts.

If you're nervous about having to rely more heavily than usual on the advice of others, you can take consolation in the fact that it's a relatively small price to pay for the great benefits that tax reform has provided. In 1987 you can pass on an unlimited amount of money to your spouse (as opposed to just $60,000 prior to 1982) without taxation, and 20 times as much money to your other heirs ($600,000, as opposed to $30,000 prior to 1982). If you should have an estate over $600,000, you can look at the cost of estate planning by experts a small price to pay for the rewards you've reaped in organizing and operating a thriving small business.

Have fun!

BUSINESS SENSE